Famous Italian Cities

Famous Italian Cities

Florence. Rome. Venice

Text by
Reinhard Bentmann and
Elisabeth Herget

translated by
J. Hendry

Cassell
London

Frontispiece:
Venice: View from the Riva della Piazzetta across the Bacino, the inner harbour-basin, towards San Giorgio Maggiore. Outstanding buildings in most other cities are grouped together in solid squares, with parks, but in Venice it is water shimmering in ever-changing light that becomes part of the city scene, so that islands, canals and buildings together form an endless unity.

CASSELL LTD.
35 Red Lion Square, London WC1R 4SG
and at Sydney, Auckland, Toronto, Johannesburg,
an affiliate of
Macmillan Publishing Co., Inc.,
New York

First published in Great Britain 1978

ISBN 0 304 30194 9

Filmset by Keyspools Ltd., Golborne, Lancashire
Printed in Italy by Arnoldo Mondadori Editore, Verona

Contents

Introduction

'In the beginning was the city'. Any general history of culture could well start off in this way, since the sources of traditional history, based on documentary evidence and excavations, have close links with the rise of city culture. 'City' means a marking-off from the 'country'; a division of labour and, eventually, manufactures and industrial production; specialisation in vital functions; organized trade; organized administration and defence; law as a binding force. It is synonymous, in a comprehensive, modern sense, with politics. To the peasant, livestock-breeder or hunter in antiquity the nearest line of hills, the nearest deep wood or marsh was unattainable and unconquerable, a 'pathless unknown'. To the townsman of early times, however, his 'locale' was the starting-point for other town-like locales, which he tried to reach by caravan or by water.

The basics of city-building lead us us back beyond 5000 B.C. to Ancient China, India (the Indus Valley cultures), Egypt and the Near East. The oldest of such settlements that can be dated, in the area that concerns us, the Mediterranean, are Jericho (9000 B.C.) and Damascus. These still exist today.

It was the politics of the city-state that took first place when the national and cultural body-politic, in our sense, was coming into being. Our word 'politics' derives from the word for city, *polis*.

This fact becomes particularly clear in the ancient Mediterranean cultures, Italy above all, which developed from the nucleus of one single city—Rome.

The idea of the city-state assumed concrete form, of global significance, on three occasions in European history: in Ancient Greece, Ancient Rome, and the Italy of the Late Middle Ages and Renaissance. The modern era begins with the transition from the Late Middle Ages to Early Renaissance. 'Modern' implies a specific rationalistic early bourgeois consciousness. That turning-point in history is therefore inconceivable in the absence of an urban way of life, which in Italy became concentrated within the focal area of our triad of cities. Florence, Rome and Venice eclipsed in splendour the peninsula's remaining metropolitan centres and in cultural and political matters, as well as in historical durability, put even such places as Milan, Bologna, Naples and Genoa in the shade.

'Town air makes you free' was a popular saying in the Middle Ages. It was unquestionably the shape that urban society, economy and culture took which provided the basis for any and every form of spiritual and political emancipation. Florence, Rome and Venice are the living proof. The peculiar feature of these three centres was the political, economic and cultural climate characterising them, at times equally, in the areas of freedom, progressive outlook, and intensity of purpose. At the same time the *genius loci* which was non-interchangeable, the political and cultural milieu, differentiated all three cities with equal sharpness as individual personalities, just as happened in Greece, permeated by the idea of the *polis,* in the case of Athens, Sparta, Corinth, Miletus and Ephesus. Jacob Burckhardt has defined the Italian Renaissance as the 'discovery [actually re-discovery] of the world and of Man' and a cultural process therefore with which only the Enlightenment in France and Germany, that pre-revolutionary phase prior to 1789, can be compared.

The development of a national Italian style via a return to native sources, the native national or, so to speak, classical culture and history of antiquity, took place chiefly within the Florence, Rome and Venice triad. Thence the movement spread over the Alps to Northern and Western Europe as an accepted European style. This national style is illustrated to a greater extent in architecture, sculpture and painting than in the literature, philosophy and music of the time. All three cities constitute a visible illustration, a 'history book in pictures', of which this book, it is hoped, will provide a significant cross-section.

What differentiated these three cities, and what have they in common? That must be our basic query. Of all three, Florence looks most to the North, Venice to the East, and Rome to the South. For all its Mediterranean character, Florence seems most like home to the traveller from the North, comparable to Verona, on account of its many medieval features. Small wonder that Goethe failed to find 'his' Italy there.

Rome, geographical centre of the peninsula, stands for Southern and Mediterranean Italy. The Roman High Renaissance and Roman Baroque, the Mediterranean contribution to the modern cultural history of Europe, could not have occurred elsewhere in this shape and form. It is no accident that the message of Italian Baroque was carried to France (Paris, the Louvre and Versailles) by the 'most Roman' of all the artists of the period, Bernini, just as a century earlier the Italian Masters Primaticcio, Leonardo da Vinci and Serlio, as guests of François I, had conveyed the new art of the Renaissance to Fontainebleau.

Lastly Venice, as the geographical position of this 'amphibious' creation, between land and water, makes clear, for centuries remained almost completely cut off from the rest of Italy. It turned across the sea to the Adriatic coast opposite, to the Aegean, the Southern and Eastern Mediterranean, the Balkans and the Levant. Throughout the Middle Ages, and even in the fifteenth and early sixteenth centuries, places like Constantinople, Athens, Patras, Rhodes, Crete, Cyprus, Damascus, Alexandria and Cairo lay nearer for Venice than Rome, Florence or Genoa. In orientation, it was old Byzantium that Venice looked to, throughout both the early and mature phases of its history. Up until modern times the city also enjoyed a special 'East Roman' status in the matter of ecclesiastical policy, liturgy and religious art, with a Patriarch, and a rite recalling the Byzantine. The striking architectural grouping of St. Mark's and the free-standing Campanile resembles a large, multi-cupola mosque with its minaret, or a Greek or Russian church, rather than a West European religious structure. Equally, the different geographic setting helps to explain the Gothic interior of Florence cathedral, or the abundance of light and space inside St. Peter's in Rome.

Rome, with the Papal States in central Italy, is an example of a theocratic system, with priestly government and spiritual power, which was compelled to assume the form of political power in order to remain a 'power' at all.

Venice never knew kings or princes, nor a real nobility, and yet it had no real republican system of government either. Instead it had a social order which had been preserved for centuries and never altered: an oligarchy of a few families, qualified for the Senate, which in their turn produced the Doge; in other words, it was a dynastic system, 'by the backdoor'. In Venice economics invariably took precedence over politics, and capital over political theory. In that sense it was the most 'modern' of the three Italian cities with which we are concerned. As a commercial and maritime state, its place lay with Genoa and Pisa, among Italy's most important 'overseas' colonial forces. We might indeed assert that Florence is the *country,* always struggling for access to the sea. Rome is mountain, *river* and port, occupying a central position, with the hilly Papal States as hinterland: it nestles within a great loop of the Tiber, with a distant but easily reached seaport in the region of Ostia. But Venice is the *sea,* and as a city an assembly of 'stone ships', floating palaces and houseboats.

Florence

The history of Florence goes back to the very roots of Italian culture. Originally an important Etruscan town, the place was a flourishing seat even in Roman times, and called 'the Flourishing', *'Fiorentia',* Italianised to *Firenze*. Even to-day a glance at the city-plan will reveal the crossed streets of the old camp *(Castrum)*. The centuries have chiselled away at the features of this most individual of Italian cities, along with Rome, Venice, Naples and Milan. Behind the modern industrious image with its elegant human types, swift in intelligence, its columns of cars and streams of tourists, its fashion industry and administrative complexes, there looms the stately face of the Renaissance city and the grave mien of the medieval *commune*. The soul of Florence still has a Northern European quality in many ways and yet is intermingled with the full resonance of Roman life. Thus arose the mixture which in his as yet vague and conventionalised picture of Italy at the beginning of his *Italian Journey* so irritated Goethe that he took leave of Florence after a few hours, on his sentimental excursion to 'his own' Arcadian Italy, which he hoped to find in Rome, with its ancient world of ruins, its artistic and political *Grandezza*, its multi faceted contours, its *Italianità* and 'Roman-ness'. Rome may be more serene, more Mediterranean and more monumental, while in Milan or Turin the pulse of Italian commerce beats faster and Venice is more fairy-like, more exotic, less sober; but to-day, just as in the eighteenth century when that Northern European movement in the

Page 8:
1 Florence: General view, showing the Arno and heart of the old city from the Piazzale Michelangelo. This glimpse of one of the most unforgettable city-scapes in the world takes in approximately the area covered by the Roman 'Florentia', beyond which medieval Florence scarcely expanded. From left to right the following landmarks can be seen: the Tower and battlements of the Palazzo Vecchio, by Arnolfo di Cambio, the marble-bright, tent-shaped roof of the San Giovanni Baptistery, the tower of the Bargello Palace (enclosed in scaffolding when the photo was taken) and, in between, the Campanile of the Santa Maria del Fiore Cathedral, built in 1334 with Giotto's co-operation; lastly, Brunelleschi's celebrated Dome (1434), the 'Roof of Florence' and the beginning of Early Renaissance architecture in Italy.

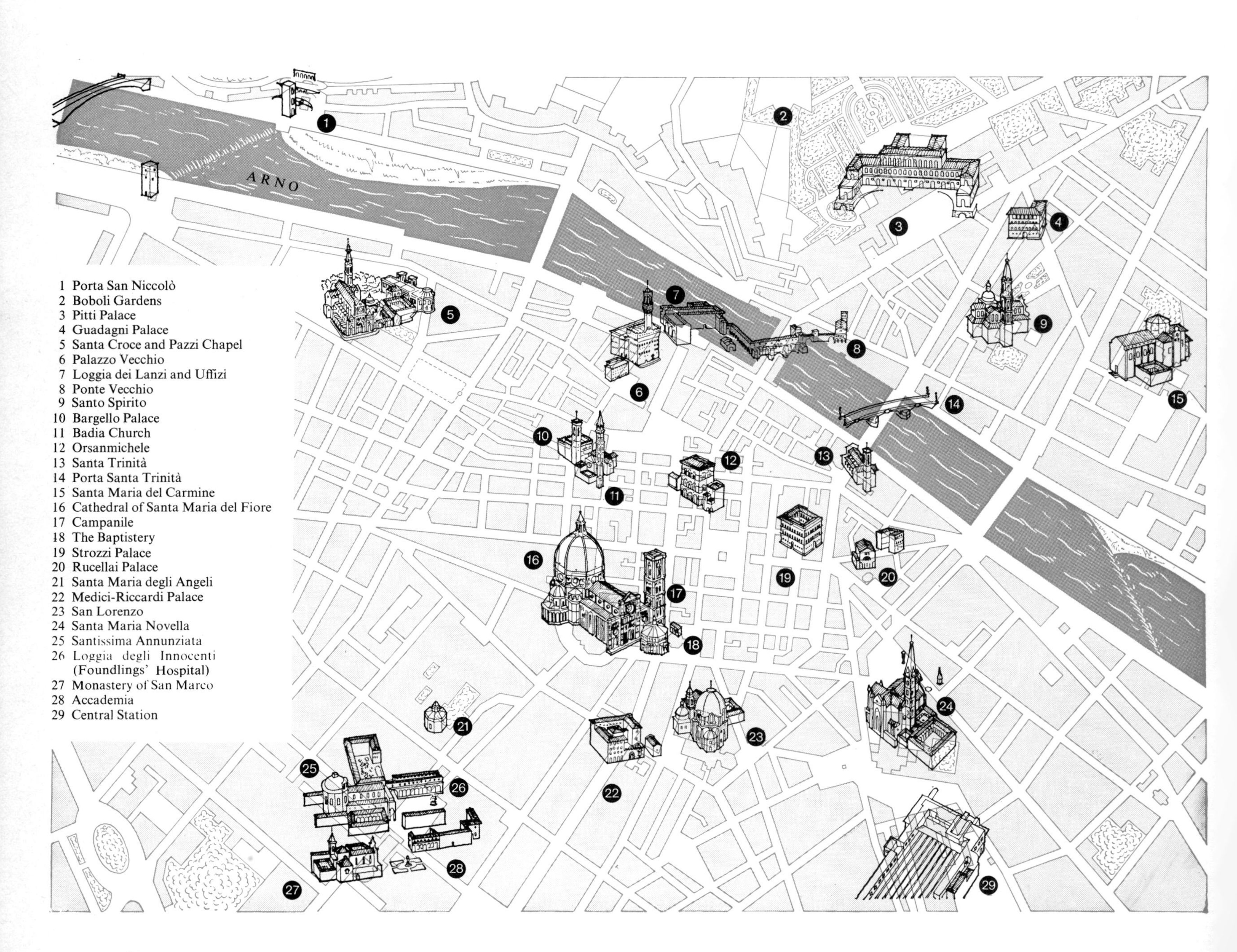

direction of educational tours to Italy began which was to introduce Italian art and culture into England and Germany, Florence still remains one of the capitals in the world of educational tourism, particularly the English, German and Scandinavian varieties, and is the Alpha and Omega of most Italian art tours. A feeling of optimism comes over one on reading the history of the houses at the beginning and end of the venerable Ponte Vecchio (Plate 26) which, though they fit neatly into the overall picture, are immediately recognizable as post-war constructions. The 1944 German retreat before the Allies led through Florence on account of its key position in communications. To halt the rolling advance of U.S. armour, the German general was ordered by the High Command on August 3, 1944 to blow up all the Arno bridges. He hesitated, however, when it came to the Ponte Vecchio. Could one simply blow sky-high a monument of the stature of the Rialto Bridge in Venice, or the Angel Bridge in Rome? The earliest mention of which was in 1177, and which later, in 1570, had been provided by the great Vasari with a corridor connecting with the Uffizi and the Pitti Palace? The lesser evil was chosen. The houses at the bridgeheads were pulled down to form a tank obstacle. The bridge was saved, the houses soon rebuilt, and after the war, the city of Florence paid tribute to its German general with a detailed citation. Similar international concern and similar respect for the spirit of the city and its historical treasures was demonstrated by the world when, following the devastation due to the catastrophic flooding of 1963, money, technical equipment and qualified restorers were summoned from every country in the world in a wave of unparalleled solidarity, to assist in the campaign of salvage.

Let us take a look at the history of Florence.

Classical Antiquity and the Middle Ages

In 9 B.C. the first peasants, fishermen and traders of what is known as the Villanovan culture settled here on the banks of the Arno, the site of modern Florence. This fact has been confirmed by recent discoveries made in the Piazza della Repubblica. The area still had no name and was of no significance, since it stood in the shadow of a flourishing hill settlement in nearby Fiesole, which dates from 500 B.C. and has now been incorporated into the city.

The Roman conquest of Italy, which began in the third century B.C., soon reached the north, and Fiesole. To begin with the hill stronghold was left untouched. A camp was set up at the river-crossing and from there the fortified Etruscan town was eventually starved into surrender. Veterans of Caesar's wars, who had been granted the privilege of creating advance defensive towns by the Settlement Law of 59 B.C. (Gallia Cisalpina—northern Italy and parts of central Italy—was still regarded as colonial territory at that date), founded a colony called 'Florentia' on the right bank of the Arno.

It was laid out in roughly the same way as the usual *Castrum.* Strictly speaking the *castrum*-city proper was supposed to be built on a rectangular plan, but the ground plan of colonial Florence was atypical, since the presence of the marshy river plain resulted in its taking on a trapezoid shape. Yet the layout did still follow the standard system, with its two main axes, the *cardo maximus* and the *decumanus,* intersecting at the central *forum* or main square and ending in four gates with watchtowers set in the city wall. Today the Roman intersection is marked by the Via Strozzi, the Via degli Speziali and the Via del Corso (the *cardo maximus*) and the Via Porta Santa Maria, the Via Calimalia and the Via Roma (the *decumanus*). Archaeologists have also accurately pinpointed the walls and gates of the ancient town, and the shape and site of the old forum can still be picked out in the Piazza della Repubblica.

The city rapidly grew and soon had all the trappings considered obligatory in the Roman Empire. It was indeed modelled on Rome itself, with the gentle line of hills on the banks of the Arno reminiscent of Rome's famous Seven Hills. The forum was surrounded by colonnades and on the artificially banked up Capitol hill stood a large temple dedicated to the official local divinity, Jupiter Optimus Maximus. Near the medieval town hall, the Palazzo Vecchio, the foundations of a classical theatre have been excavated and thermal baths have been found, while outside the walls lay an amphitheatre designed on an oval plan. Near the Baptistery beside the Duomo excavations have shown that the fitments in the dwellings and palaces of Imperial Florence were truly magnificent. Beautiful floor mosaics covering large surfaces and quite unharmed came to light and were seen to equal the finest inlay work in Rome and Pompei. These are important discoveries because in the fifteenth and sixteenth centuries Renaissance art and culture would consciously hark back to the cultural and architectural history of ancient Florentia, with a typically Florentine feeling for tradition, continuity and local pride.

Virtually nothing was left of the ancient ruins, so the situation is very different from Rome, where even today the layout of the palaces, theatres and squares can still be made out, sometimes on several levels.

From early sources we know that as late as about 1300 a classical equestrian statue still stood near the Ponte Vecchio. The great Dante must surely have often walked past it. This gives us some idea of the concept of the grandeur and dignity of classical antiquity that he derived from the chance survival of what was most probably a third-rate example of 'mass-production' in provincial Rome, since he was not familiar with any comparable examples of a higher quality. Following subsequent flooding of the Arno the statue was lost, but it must have seemed important to the people of the 'pre-Renaissance' period, something rather special, or else they would not have handed down the fact of its existence. The same applies to our knowledge of the fact that in about 800 A.D. an equestrian statue dating from classical antiquity stood in front of Charlemagne's palace in Aachen (Aix-la-Chapelle), a visible proof that the Carolingian era saw the birth of the concept of Empire.

This dearth of monuments from their own idealized past in no way troubled the Florentines of the fourteenth and fifteenth centuries, however. Their feeling for history lacked any scientific basis and was refreshingly artless, so that the products of local builders in the Middle Ages were simply declared to be 'classical'. Brunelleschi, like Dante, considered the Florentine Baptistery to be an ancient temple.

City chronicles provide only rare and vague reports concerning the 'dark' transition period. This is true equally of most of Italy's ancient centres. Some account is given of the 250 A.D. martyrdom of San Miniato in the reign of Emperor Decius, a sign of early attempts at Christianization, and strong reaction on the part of the state authorities, as happened all over the Mediterranean territories of the Orbis Romanus. A Florence bishopric is reported from the early fourth century A.D. Then, at the close of the century, in 393 A.D., St. Ambrose, Bishop of Milan, consecrated before the gates of the old town the original structure of San Lorenzo, which, in time if not in importance, ranks alongside the first great 'chief basilicas', in Rome and Milan, of the declining Imperium Romanum.

In the historically 'lost' period, between the fourth and fifth centuries, fluctuating waves of migration passed over Florence, but it remained free of the corpse-robbers of the Roman Empire, owing to its excellent system of communications. Martially-minded, and disliking towns, these migrants left behind no architectural or cultural traces worthy of mention, but did leave heaps of ash. The Goths arrived at the beginning of the fifth century; the Byzantines in 539; and the Longobards about 570. The once brilliant city had shrunk to an insignificant shell, while the decimated population numbered only a few hundred. It was the time of a general return to peasant conditions, which has rightly been called 'the hibernation of the urban social system'. When threatened, the inhabitants all took refuge in the old Roman theatre,

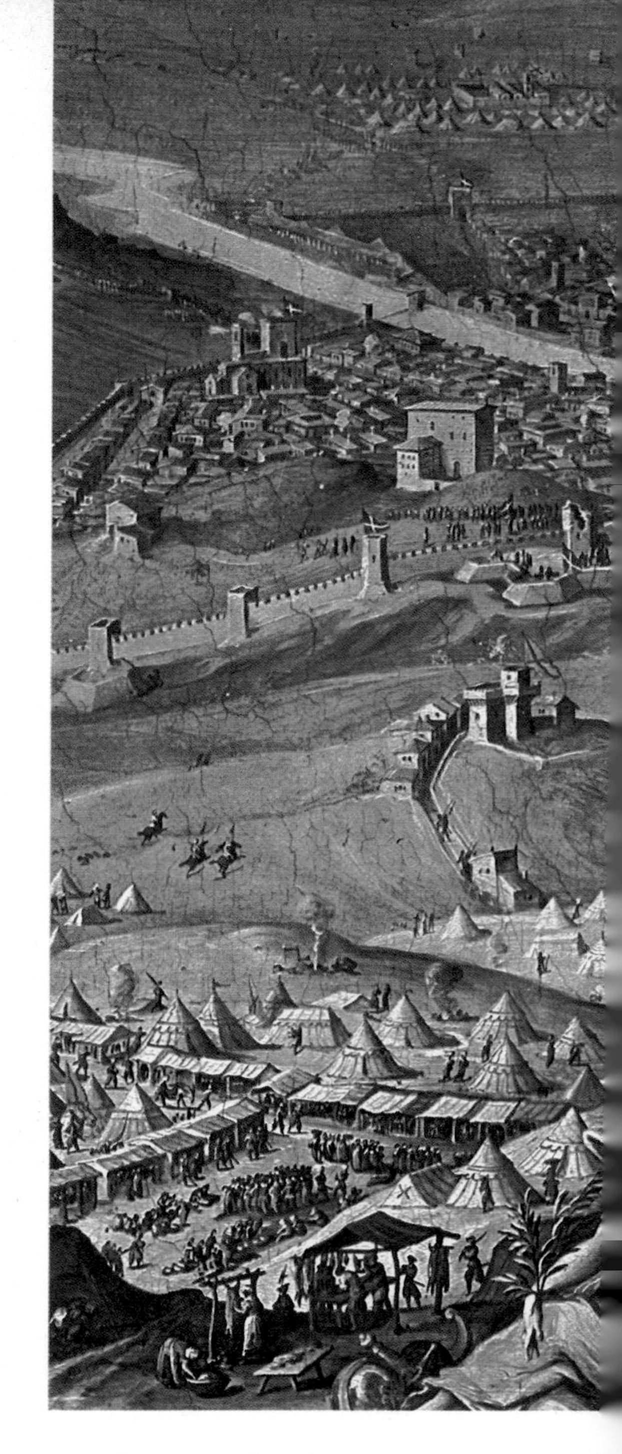

2 Unknown artist from the group surrounding Giorgio Vasari: A view of sixteenth-century Florence, with encampment: Palazzo Vecchio. In the late sixteenth century Vasari and his circle painted several rooms in the Palazzo Vecchio, among them the 'Room of the Five Hundred' (Salone dei Cinquecento), the place of assembly for the Standing Conference of Representatives of the People. Large frescoes depict the history of Florence and the Medici, especially the wars against Siena and Pisa. These play an important part in the history of realistic battle-scenes. In content, the picture shown fits into the context of such detailed historical 'snapshots'. It portrays an important moment in history: the siege of Florence by the German mercenaries of Emperor Charles V, after the notorious 'Sacco di Roma', the sack of Rome, in 1527. Florence burrowed into its defences at this time, with the assistance of the fortress engineer Michelangelo, and was able to purchase immunity from plunder on the part of the undisciplined foreign invaders by paying a ransom of 80,000 talers. Otherwise the consequences for Florence's art treasures would have been too terrible to contemplate. The background shows an authentic panorama of Florence with the Arno, the dome Palazzo

2

Vecchio, Badia Church and Bargello Palace. The completely preserved city wall of 1172 with the (earlier) wall surrounding the outlying suburb on the southern bank of the Arno. On the right, in front of the city, the monastery of the Olivetans, with the Church of San Miniato, surrounded by a modern constellation of strongpoints. During the 1527 battles the monastery held a key position as an advanced outpost. It was strongly fortified under Michelangelo, who, in order to protect the half-finished campanile from enemy fire, covered the lower with straw mattresses, one of the earliest examples of wartime protection of cultural property. On one of the hills a fortified German battery can be seen, with large towers made of brushwood fascines and modern gun carriages, conducting an artillery duel with the Florentine battery in San Miniato. The entire city is surrounded by lanes of tents belonging to the investing German forces, and there are genre-like tableaux of camp-life in this period of mercenary troops.

which had been converted into a fortress.

This Florentine 'Theatre Fort' was later given a strong defensive tower, the first indication of a strengthening city identity. There lay the nucleus of the later communal authority, and there, about 1300, arose the Palazzo della Signoria (Palazzo Vecchio), which adopted from the old city fortifications the theme of the proudly erect tower that remains even to-day the city's symbol and landmark (Plate 16).

At the opposite pole to secular rule in the early Middle Ages stood the ecclesiastical district, with the bishop's residence, near the present cathedral of Santa Maria del Fiore.

But all was still on a modest scale. Florentine chronicles begin again with the High Middle Ages. Twelfth and thirteenth century scribes link the city's rebirth with that most illustrious of figures (from their point of view)—Charlemagne. Legend reports, with patriotic exaggeration, on the liberation and re-establishment of Florence from the alleged yoke of the 'barbarians' in the latter part of the eighth century. What is historically accurate is that the city recovered its status as an independent and self-assured commune, but this only in the ninth century, and all we can be sure of is that Charlemagne on his first visit to Rome in 786 attended Christmas Matins, donated generously to the local churches and monasteries, and was later to stay in the city from time to time.

In the tenth century, while the Italian kingdom was weakened by the ambitions of men like Berengar, Adalbert and Arduin of Ivrea, the March of

3

4 Florence: San Miniato al Monte: Façade. The church lies on a hill outside the town, on the south bank of the Arno, and was built to commemorate the city's most eminent saint, St. Miniatus, who suffered martyrdom in 250 A.D. in Florence, under Emperor Decius. The original chapel over the tomb was probably built on the site of the present church, Florence's oldest Christian sanctuary. The church is famed for its façade, in the finest style of Florentine 'incrustation', with light and dark marble plaques in strict geometric pattern, and is a masterpiece of the Florentine Proto-Renaissance style (1075). Stylistically the façade is closely related to the marble incrustation of the Bel San Giovanni, *the Florentine Baptistery (1060).*

3 Florence: A view through the battlements of the 1172 city wall towards the two most outstanding landmarks, the Palazzo Vecchio tower, by Arnolfo di Cambio (from 1298), and Brunelleschi's dome (from 1434).

4 Tuscia, bordered to the south by the 'Patrimonium Petri', 'the Papal State', and to the north-east by the Romagna-Pentapolis, pushed northwards with a spur of territory as far as Mantua, and was able to acquire a stable position in Central Italy as a factor making for political order. Florence was and remained the centre, and centre also of that great split into two great political parties, which was to have such a fateful influence on Italy's subsequent medieval history, and ultimately delay the creation of an Italian nation until the nineteenth century. These factions were the Ghibellines (so called after the Hohenstaufen town of Waiblingen) and the Guelphs, or respectively those who looked to the north and were loyal to the Emperor, and those who looked to Rome and were faithful to the Pope. This split occurred as early as the year 1000, and was the result of controversy between the Italian 'national king', Arduin of Ivrea, and the German Emperor, Henry II. The succeeding centuries are marked by rapid and, even for the expert historian, almost inextricable confusion, with first one camp and then the other emerging victorious throughout the history of Tuscia, or Tuscany. The most prominent victim of this unhappy quarrel was Florence's greatest son, Dante Alighieri (1265–1321).

With the Ottonian emperors, the city came under the influence of the 'Empire across the Alps' and so attained its first flowering. The important Tuscan Margrave Hubert and his son Hugo at the turn of the century followed a realistic policy as between two great powers, Emperor and Pope. Their skilful manoeuvring between 'blocks', with some emphasis on the imperial idea, began to pay off, and the results of Florentine diplomacy were to be seen in the city's wealth of ecclesiastical and secular monuments, paid for in part by the foreign powers concerned in the form of gifts. In every period, including the Early and High Middle Ages, calculation was a Florentine characteristic, political balance being directly related to the balance of payments, and political roulette played in the manner of a player who invariably carries with him a ready-reckoner and a table to show the potential profits. Jacob Burckhardt, referring to the fourteenth and fifteenth centuries, has rightly termed Florence and Venice the 'home of statistics'.

The Proto-Renaissance Period

The eleventh century in Florence was characterized by an initial, medieval 'renovatio' in architecture, the Proto-Renaissance style, a particular form of European Romanesque, and the first international style to succeed the Graeco-Roman. Examples from this period such as the original San Lorenzo, San Piero Scheraggio, Santa Felicità, Santa Reparata, and the Badia Fiorentina, have mostly perished, or been overlaid by newer constructions. The shape of these spacious basilicas with aisles can however be inferred from San Miniato al Monte (Plate 4), and the Badia Fiorentina. It was the Baptistery above all, however, which survived unscathed as brilliant testimony to Florentine Romanesque. It ranks as one of the finest buildings in Europe.

The overriding principle of this style is that the surface of the entire structure, smoothly and artlessly built-up, is given a covering of precious marble plaques. The thin but valuable panels surround the building like a skin, and stretch tightly over it, in the membrane-fashion. The decorative and practical nature of this technique, known also as the incrustation style, is manifest in some Florentine churches, where the façade, splendidly clad in light and dark plaques, stands in front of a rough stone basilica which has remained undressed, thus giving the façade the appearance of some decorative wall or a magnificent marble panel, thrust, so to speak, like a slab, in front of the edifice.

Today's traveller to the East is confronted with this same style—in miniature—as soon as he takes up one of the small inlaid wooden caskets that are proffered from the Lebanon to Morocco as souvenirs in bazaars. The smooth surface of the wood is inlaid all over with abstract, geometric designs

6

Pages 16 and 17:
*5 Florence: The Cathedral of Santa Maria del Fiore. Almost all the important Florentine artists of the Late Middle Ages and Early Renaissance took part in the cathedral's construction, which began in 1296: Arnolfo di Cambio (until 1301 Director of the Project); F. Talenti (from 1357 onwards); Giotto (Campanile, from 1334); Andrea Pisano (Campanile, 1336–1348); Orcágna and Brunelleschi (the Dome, 1434–1461). After being frequently brought to a halt, the work was finally completed with the aid of the wealthy and powerful Wool-Weavers Guild (Arte della Lana) as a symbol of civil pride. It became known throughout the world not merely owing to Brunelleschi's outstanding Dome, the 'Roof of Florence', the first piece of Renaissance architecture in Italy, but also on account of the magnificent marble incrustation, along the lines of the Florentine Proto-Renaissance style (Baptistery, San Miniato). The white marble is from Carrara, the green from Prato (*verde di Prato*) and the red from the Maremma (*rosso di Maremma*). Originally the church was called Santa Reparata, but about 1300 the municipal authorities changed the name by decree to Santa Maria 'del Fiore', to harmonise with the old name of the city, 'Florentia'. This was a way of announcing that, in accordance with ancient custom, the Blessed Virgin was now the divinity looking after both city and state, or the 'Tyche' (the Greek goddess of Fortune) of Florence.*

6 Florence: Cathedral of Santa Maria del Fiore: Campanile (Bell-tower). The history of the bell-tower is closely connected with that of the Cathedral. From 1334 to 1337 Giotto was in charge of the work, and thereafter, until 1348 or 1350, Andrea Pisano. The cupola originally planned to top the structure never in fact materialized, but the tower is generally held to be the loveliest campanile in Italy, its picturesque appearance being due to the happy conjunction of architectural and graphic elements. The strict architectural form combines perfectly with the clear division into storeys and the imaginative treatment of the surface by means of marble incrustations and a series of reliefs. Recent research reveals that the use of free-standing campanili, to be found only in Italy, is connected with a liturgical regulation that bells had to be used in the divine service. This trend occurs, for the first time, in the seventh century, which explains why the early Christian churches of the fourth to sixth centuries (such as Ravenna) had later to be provided with bell-towers. The custom became a tradition in later periods, as the Duomo in Florence illustrates.

in metal, mother-of-pearl, ivory or fishbone, giving the simple container the character of a treasure-chest or jewel-box, that turns everything in it, even only a few coins, into something valuable. It is therefore most appropriate that the Florentines should have affectionately named 'their' baptistery the 'Treasure-Chest' of the city on the Arno. Dante calls the Baptistery *"il bel San Giovanni",* after its patron, St. John.

Concerning the origins of this style as many contradictory theories abound as there are writers on art. It has no real parallel, either in Italy (Pisa for example) or in the rest of Europe. All we can say is that it seems to be a specifically Florentine invention, which appears suddenly before us, fully-developed, in the eleventh century.

One possible explanation lies in the architectonic legacy left by antiquity. Roman buildings, too, unlike the Greek, had been largely erected in this manner since the first century B.C. At that time shuttering was discovered, and how to face a 'cement' base with conventionally built-up bands of tiles, or ashlar. The technical Roman expression for this was *opus caementicium.* It consisted of a firmly-baked mass of mortar, with other compounds and rubble, or crushed brick. The rough or cement base was then faced with thin marble plaques, and fastened with bronze clamps to form the building's actual façade.

In the High Middle Ages many Roman monuments on Italian soil must have had this marble facing, so that the Florentine incrustation technique was following familiar classical models. This explains why as early as the thirteenth and fourteenth centuries the Baptistery could be mistaken for and idealized as a slightly altered classical building, or a Roman temple to Mars.

The link with Ancient Rome can be brought closer still in the Baptistery, as has already been mentioned. Valuable floor mosaics dating from the Roman period have been discovered recently in the foundations. This mosaic work must have become apparent to the architects of the time, during the excavations in the eleventh century for the new baptistery. That the work was not destroyed by the medieval builders but merely filled in and built over can either be regarded as an early example of conservation or ascribed to the Florentine feeling for tradition, and local sensibility as regards the *'genius loci'.* The Roman mosaics certainly stimulated the imagination of the Masters of the Florentine Baptistery.

What is peculiar about the Baptistery, however, is that here—at the very start of an independent local art—we can already grasp the essential features which subsequently mark the Florentine style up to the fifteenth and sixteenth centuries, i.e. a rational and at times inflexible spirit, which could be called dry and unimaginative were it not a consequence of the Florentine feeling for artistic discipline, mastery of form, economy of shape and shrewd judgement in the application of artistic media. We can imagine the typical Florentine artist of any period as wielding setsquare and ready-reckoner, rather than as some early Bohemian with velvet cap and bow. The people of Florence were apt to reverse the saying: 'Life is earnest and art gay', for to them art and culture were never the décor and background to living, but its very heart and soul.

Roman art with its overwhelming richness of form and imaginative décor, its tendency towards large-scale and often strident effects, plus its grandiose and theatrical or architectonic setting, was as foreign to the Florentine as the graphically delicate nuances of Venetian art, with its golden decorative scheme that sparkled in the half-light, and was as closely wrought as a carpet, conveying the effect of some fresco in a Byzantine church, or of some piece of booty from the gorgeous tent of the Great Khan, exotic, oriental, un-Italian in essence, and broken up by the light diffused across the lagoon into soft nuances free of shadow. The sky above Florence is not as radiant and blue as the sky over Rome, and the air is not as damp and oppressive as in Venice. Thomas Mann's celebrated novel about death could have taken place only in Venice, not in Rome, and certainly not in Florence.

If we compare the important medieval churches in the three cities, St.

Peter's predecessor in Rome, St. Mark's in Venice and the Duomo and Baptistery grouping in Florence, we are at once struck by the marked difference of spirit between them even in medieval times. In the old St. Peter's we have a multipartite complicated organization of architectural masses and great spaces, laid out on long, extensive axes, and all-comprehensive and cosmopolitan in conception; in St. Mark's, a dense shape and colour texture which is difficult to penetrate, consisting of cupolas and bits and pieces, with every surface, even the tiniest corner, full of ornamentation; a creation foreign to the European world which has settled down here like some powerful, mythological creature from the Orient (Plates 93 and 107).

Florence is totally different. The artistic imagination here is tempered, and the formal effect carefully calculated. It must never become a matter of course, overwhelm or get out of control. Formal concepts and morphological inventions are given clear delineation, and react independently on one another. Florentine art knows nothing of the fortuitous, nothing of picturesque effects, or pastoral nooks. Uniquely inspired artistic ideas and spontaneous creations are suspect until they have been confirmed by academic theory, and tested in a long series of practical works. Otherwise the so-called inspiration could have been pure chance.

This is why the Florentines have always proved better at graphic work and design, like the Germans and Northerners. The city has produced magnificent sculpture, in both stone and bronze, characteristically graphic and linear in conception, but has been poor in great painting talent. It was in Florence that (with Donatello) the doctrine of *disegno,* or drawing, was first developed. *Disegno* and draughtsmanship remain constants in Florentine art that override the centuries.

All these features are revealed in the Baptistery. The ground-plan and elevation display a Latin rationality and a kind of Gallic *clarté*. The original structure has the air of a purely Euclidean, geometric body, which states no more in the ground-plan than it does in the formation of the façade; speaks no differently internally than it does externally; and has no ambition to mean any more than it is—an accumulating architectonic crystal, a great prism in the centre of the area covered by the immunity of the Bishop of Florence. In

7 Florence: The Cathedral of Santa Maria del Fiore: Campanile, the bas-reliefs on the rectangular base at the East Side. The original design for these reliefs probably goes back to Giotto and constitutes an ingenious display of the entire doctrine of scholasticism, as relating to society and salvation. The historical and symbolic illustrations call to mind the complicated images decorating the Gothic cathedrals of France. Those shown are the lower reliefs by Andrea Pisano and his School (about 1340). From left to right they represent: 1. Navigation; 2. Hercules with a conquered Giant; 3. Agriculture and 4. Chariot racing.

7

its abstraction and at the same time in its deep sensuousness, the building could be described as an architectonic Utopia become a reality, or as an expression in stone of the nature of architecture.

The High Middle Ages

The eleventh century in Florence was characterized in an architectural as well as a political sense by a launching out on to new paths. The town nobles organized on rigid lines and began to gain in influence. They and their economically dependent 'clientèle' formed into solid communities, by street or family, as was a custom in medieval Tuscany, and the powerful defence works in the city, with their high fortified towers, gave significant expression to that fact. Their fascinating town silhouettes are familiar to us from ancient descriptions and pictorial illustrations. The heart of the city, with over eighty such towers, must have presented even in the thirteenth century a significant picture, like a forest of lances, or the skyline of some modern city, with slender towers of skyscrapers. The Palazzo Vecchio (Plate 16) gives some impression of how it all originally looked, as does the centre of San Gimignano in Southern Tuscany, which has been preserved in its medieval form and is one of the most rewarding places in Italy to visit. In Florence nothing of the kind survived, apart from a few remains built into modern structures. Yet in the thirteenth century already the violent party struggles between noble families was beginning to bring down almost entirely that 'forest of towers'. It was in the fifteenth century that by a decree of state the usurping dynasty of the Medici ordained that the towers still standing be torn down. The arrogant claim to power so tangible in these architectural symbols must have proved intolerable to the Medici, who had seized power.

In the twelfth century, Florence's fluctuating course between Pope and Emperor lent such an impulse to the city that the population expanded beyond the confines of the Roman Gastrum Square. The ancient surrounding wall, until then still largely preserved, was taken down, and a larger one put up. The city was also surrounded on three sides by wide moats, while on the fourth the Arno served as a natural defence.

Florence began to develop into an Italian and then a European centre of trade, acquiring an important place in early metropolitan commercial capitalism. Business relations spread across the whole of Europe and also 'overseas', which then meant the Eastern Mediterranean, the Levant, North Africa and the Black Sea. Following the Spanish *Reconquista,* Arab rule in the Central Mediterranean began to collapse from the eleventh century onwards, and the crusades, with their world-wide political and economic repercussions, did likewise. Into the vacuum stepped the Italian commercial cities Genoa, Pisa, Naples, Venice and Florence. Like Venice, the Florence region became one of the first 'industrial landscapes' in Europe, and European and Middle East trade, still largely operating on the basis of barter, was at once the cause and effect of this process. Eastern goods in demand, such as silk, brocades, damask, cotton, camel hair, porcelain, dyes, spices, essences, medicines, pearls, ivory and jewels, reached Europe from Asia and the Levant, via the old caravan routes (the Silk Road) still under Arab control, there to be exchanged for finished goods from Milan, Florence, Upper Germany, Flanders and Brabant. The up-and-coming Italian communes were the governing wheels in this trade exchange in the old world, and among them Florence soon occupied a leading place.

This mercantile expansion, of course, was unlikely to produce a peaceful system of municipal government. On the contrary, it was the cause of internal struggles for power between rival forces in the trading aristocracy. The 'city peace' was forever under threat, and the conflict sharpened once the masked greed of the Florentine commercial overlords discovered that the ideal arena for their squabbles lay in foreign policy. Mutual aversion among a few city families assumed concrete form with their political division into two parties, the Ghibellines and the Guelphs. People joined these parties only partly for

9

8 Florence: The cathedral of Santa Maria del Fiore, part of the choir. Projecting structures have been placed between the three arms of the choir to take the enormous weight of Brunelleschi's Dome. The photograph on the left shows one of these, at the ends of which Brunelleschi placed semicircular exedras. It also provides a good example of the most attractive interplay of white, red and green marble arranged in geometric patterns on the façade.

9 Florence: Santa Maria Novella. The Façade. The front of Florence's most important Dominican church, begun in 1246, constitutes one of the loveliest incrustation façades in the city. it was executed from 1456 to 1470 from plans by the great Leon Battista Alberti (Portal, side pilasters and gable with side volutes). The result is a charming mélange of Medieval and Early Renaissance forms. The gable architrave bears the founder's name in large classical lettering: 'IOHANES. ORICELLARIUS' and the final date 'MCCCCLXX' (1470).

political reasons, expressed in shouts of: 'The Emperor!' 'The Pope!' The aim was rather to eliminate annoying business competition and get within reach of certain trade privileges and monopolies which the feuding Emperor and Pope were both in a position to distribute. Whenever competitor X deprived competitor Y of the right of pre-emption for a bale of silk or load of pepper, obscenities, directed at a Guelph or Ghibelline patronised by Emperor or Pope, would be hurled from tower to tower under the cover of a shower of arrows; premises would be looted; and nightly brawls take place in the local taverns, among the bodyguards of the various *torri*, who were easily recognisable dressed as they were in the family-colours.

It was this picture of a city rent by internal dissension that writers like Petrarch (1304–1374) and Boccaccio (1313–1375) had before them when they set the ideal of country villas and estates against this distorted and perverted town life, or when, in the style of Roman writers like Cato, Cicero and Columnella, they called on people to return to an utopian pastoral existence. Using expressions such as *brutalità*, *perversità* e *scandolo* (brutality, perversion and scandal) they lashed out at town life as sum-total of every private and political vice, so that when at last the Black Death, the Plague, entered the narrow streets of the medieval city, no longer a harbour for citizens but only for gloomy secrets, and ruled by spies and murdering

10 Florence: Santa Croce: General view, West façade and Campanile. Church and Monastery, one of the most powerful Franciscan foundations in Italy, and founded ostensibly by St. Francis himself, were begun in 1295 and completed in 1385. The incrustation façade remained a fragment. It is nineteenth-century work, based on pseudo-Gothic seventeenth-century sketches, and was completed in 1863. The present bell-tower dates from 1842 and derives in a formal sense from the Badia Tower.

bandits, it seemed as well-merited dispensation of Providence. To Boccaccio the Plague symbolized the political conditions in a city 'sick unto death', and, in actual fact, the party-political quarrel, with its repercussions in the physical, or at least economic destruction of whatever fraction in the thirteenth and early fourteenth century lost power, *did* come to acquire that quality of 'bestialità', or bestiality, treated so movingly by Petrarch and Dante.

After 1250 A.D. the city was politically reorganized by stages, in a democratic sense. These are the glorious days of the so-called 'Primo Popolo', which entered the annals of European constitutional history as one of the first, if not *the* first democratic constitution since the antique world. The Guelph party was not of course acting without a precedent. At the height of the 'Ghibelline era' at the turn of the twelfth and thirteenth centuries the first 'democratic' revolution had occurred, when the guilds, together with the feudal supporters of the Empire, broke the power of great families, the *torri*.

By 1200 the 'New Class' of merchants was hardly distinguishable from the older, established aristocracy, in terms of political weight and economic power, and had partly intermarried with it. Behind it, the guilds were pressing strongly forward, and the two classes inevitably met head-on, as indeed they must, in an early capitalist sense: raw materials and semi-finished products reached the city through the dealers, and were left to the guilds for further processing either through orders, or by them on their own account (First profit stage). After processing, the finished products left town again through the dealers and were disposed of on world markets at a profit (Second profit stage). The upper and lower classes were dependent on each other, so that workers and small businesses could make their demands felt. One prerequisite, of course, was that the classes putting pressure on the 'New Class' should organize themselves. This occurred when the craftsmen formed into seven large guilds in the year 1173, a memorable date in European municipal and class history, and one no less significant in social history than in the history of the cultural superstructure, in other words for Florence's development into one of the first 'art cities'.

The two 'Consuls' at the head of the exclusive Merchants' Corporation had their counterpart in the guilds in the form of freely-elected 'Rectors', who looked after the business interests of their colleagues. Through a tactical coalition with the lower strata the feudal Ghibelline party was enabled temporarily to break the dominant influence of the rich merchants, who were inclined to be anti-Empire and to favour the Guelphs. The 'Emperor's Party' then had to make important political concessions to the plebeians in the form of democratic rights, which were in contradiction to feudal ideology. This was the time when the 'free citizen' came into being, to defend his vital rights henceforth in sturdy and courageous fashion, though neither a noble, nor traditionally wealthy. From 1193 on it could rightly be said in Florence that 'town air makes you free'. Paradoxically enough, the city government was for a brief period both democratic and feudal. The Podestà (Mayor) and his boards were dependent on the guilds. Podestà and City Council were responsible for the administration and military policy, but the guilds had managed to arrange that treaties, the very essence of political activity then as now, could be concluded only with the assent of their 'rectors'.

In 1260 the Ghibelline reaction once again attempted to shatter the painfully acquired peace by means of a putsch, designed to overthrow the constitution of the democratic *'Primo Popolo'*, but failed. The supporters of the Empire had to flee the city, and sought refuge with the people of Siena who invariably looked with distrust on the aspirations of Florence. But the Guelph Party unwisely let itself be lured in pursuit of the conspirators beyond the security of the city wall and suffered a crushing reverse in open country at Montaperti, which has passed into Florentine legend. In addition, denuded of defenders, the city fell into the hands of enemy units operating in the Guelph rear. At the Peace Congress of Empoli, however, the prudent Ghibelline leader, Farinata degli Uberti, succeeded in stressing moderation, thus preventing the total destruction of Florence. Otherwise the present-day visitor would probably find it much poorer, and with great gaps.

Florence then had to continue its painstaking struggle for a position within the circle of Tuscan city-states. Arezzo was finally forced to capitulate, and in 1284, by skilfully woven diplomatic intrigue, the Florentines managed to stoke the fires of conflict between Genoa and Pisa to the point where open hostilities broke out, in which the Genovese decisively defeated the Pisans at the gates of Florence. The city emerged from these conflicts strengthened, and with a consolidated political constitution. Trade and industry flourished, and the coffers of the merchants and armaments manufacturers also filled up, especially in these times of constant minor wars.

In 1293 the famous Florentine 'Ordinances of Justice', put a temporary end

11 Florence: Santa Croce. Cloisters, with Pazzi Chapel. Various elements combine here to form a grouping which is impressive in its effect. First we have the nave of undressed stone, symbol of French simplicity. These spacious preaching churches of the mendicant friars have been called 'prayer-barns'. Then comes the fourteenth century cloisters, among Florence's finest, and finally, the Pazzi Chapel, begun by Brunelleschi in 1430 as a sepulchre for the banking family of the Pazzi, who were opposed to the Medici. The upper floor of the chapel façade remained unfinished, and is topped to-day by an ugly platform roof.

12 Florence: San Lorenzo. The West façade, four-sided cupola and sacristy. San Lorenzo is one of the oldest churches in Florence, or Italy. The first ecclesiastical structure was erected as early as 380, and solemnly consecrated in 393 by St. Ambrose, Bishop of Milan. A new building was put up in 1058, which stood until the fifteenth century. New plans were worked out on the model of Santa Croce about 1418, and between 1420 and 1421 Brunelleschi took charge and set in motion work on Florence's first post-medieval church building. After his death the work was carried on by his pupil, Manetti. Shortly after 1500 Michelangelo began to devote himself to the task. In 1517 he prepared a model in clay for the façade, followed by one in wood with twenty-four wax figures. Between 1518 and 1519 he was in Carrara to break up blocks of marble for the decorative figures on the façade, but Leo X, the Medici Pope, was obliged in the end to cancel the contract, for lack of funds. This renunciation of Michelangelo's plan has been termed the 'tragedy of the façade', and it stands there today in raw and fissured condition. The church's importance lies in the Old Sacristy's internal design, Brunelleschi's first work (1419–1428), and particularly in the New Sacristy, by Michelangelo, by means of which the Master was 'compensated' for the failure of the façade project (1520–1523). It is on account of the (incomplete) statuary by Michelangelo for the Medici Tomb (1523–1534) that the New Sacristy must be numbered amongst the world's most important art sites. (c.f. Plates 57–60). This is the reason why it now bears the not quite correct name of 'Cappella Medicea' (Medici Chapel). The Medici family's extraordinary interest in the work is explained by the fact that their ancient seat, the Medici-Riccardi Palace, belonged to the Parish of San Lorenzo. San Lorenzo was thus, so to speak, the original home-parish of the Medicis, even at times when they were supplying Popes and Cardinals.

to the process of self-discovery that had lasted for more than a century, that ceaseless power and class-struggle between guild-members, patricians and nobles, and between producers, distributors and the 'old class' of feudal estate-owners. The 'popolo grosso' (commercial patricians) was finally forbidden by the constitution of 1293 to take part in any political activity. The party intrigues which kept occurring even after 1260 had led as a result at the end of the century to the irretrievable banishment of the 'Whites', the Ghibellines. In 1302 the City Governor, Cante de Gabrielli, had the opposition leaders, who were still in the city, publicly executed. His régime of terror and the cruel physical destruction of his opponents were considered legally justified in the main, in view of the continuing chaotic political conditions operating in the city. Dante, the most prominent victim of this persecution of the 'Whites', was out of the country at the time and so escaped the bloodshed. Italy indeed owes its most outstanding poetry not least to Dante's personal fate and the lament for a lost political identity, i.e. the dream of an ideal national kingdom.

The change in architecture around 1300 was visible evidence of a newly-recovered municipal identity. Architecture thereby became the ultimate medium of political expression. Nobles, guilds and city government entered into fruitful and artistically productive competition, having their own architectural conceptions. A series of monumental palaces illustrates the new style: the Bargello Palace (begun in 1255 and completed in 1346: Plate 19) originally the seat of communal administration departments; the Palazzo dell'Arte della Lana (1308), centre of the eminent Wool Weavers' Guild, which many plastic artists later joined because it was exclusive; the Palazzo di Parte Guelfa (late thirteenth century), headquarters of the Guelph Party, half-way between a trade-union and a political lobby; and lastly, that most splendid creation, the Palazzo Vecchio or Palazzo della Signoria (1298–1314, probably by Arnolfo di Cambio: Plates 16 and 17), seat of city government. These are no longer tower-like fortresses like the seats of the nobles in the High Middle Ages, but 'civil' buildings, constructed like palaces. Personal safety no longer required a fortress-city, capable of bearing arms, but was

12

guaranteed by the wall surrounding the city, and by a system of political treaties, rights and privileges. Nevertheless even the new palaces by no means gave up rampart and battlement, or the tower-overall theme and the powerful, rugged, running walls. Yet these reminders of medieval defensive constructions are now employed symbolically and for effect, since there is nothing more that requires to be physically defended inside the city walls, and the point is merely to represent and preserve abstract political 'titles', positions and privileges.

The Palazzo Vecchio amply demonstrates this. It is difficult to term the building either 'beautiful' or 'ugly', since it is entirely outside aesthetic categories such as these. The extreme concentration of the architecture is nevertheless political and 'representative', down to the smallest detail, a metaphor, in stone, of communal self-awareness. The body, defensive and hermetic as it is on the outside, in its unpolished, squared-off treatment, is yet restrained and well-proportioned. Only the upward straining of the arrogant, thrusting tower, and the duplicated theme of prominent battlement on palace and tower convey a hybrid effect. While the Campanile in Venice (Plate 107) creates the necessary counterpoint to the vast spatial composition of Piazza and Piazzetta, making them into an 'ensemble', and at the same time conferring on them order and articulation like limbs yet without subordinating itself to them, the overpowering tower-motif in Florence

13

breaks through the limited structure of medieval space. The lofty dimensions of tower and palace can scarcely be apprehended by the spectator, or reduced to corporeal terms. It is only from a distance that the Vecchio Tower can be seen in proper perspective as one of the governing features on the city horizon along with the Cathedral. (Plate 1). Mention has been made for this reason of the almost 'rude majesty' of the structure (J. M. Wiesel 1956) and, logically enough, in eighteenth and nineteenth century English architecture reference was made to creations like the Palazzo Vecchio when building assignments came up involving comparable demands in the matter of representation. This illustrative architecture has become a mirror-image of internal and external political positions and claims, and excludes in its apparently North European *robustezza* any interpretation as an expression of Roman or Italian character. By comparison, the Town Halls of the late medieval and the Renaissance periods in Flanders, Brabant or Upper Germany, must occupy a

13 Florence: Santo Spirito. Construction was begun in 1436 under Brunelleschi who died in 1446 a few days before the roof-vaulting started. His successors were unable to reach any unified conception, and the façade remained as it was, to be completed later in its existing rather tedious form. Brunelleschi planned to place pillars at the front, with an opulent four-portal grouping. The flanking gable volutes are a late baroque addition, while the present, smooth plaster-work dates from 1957. The campanile, one of the most elegant in the city, goes back to Brunelleschi but was completed only in 1566.

14 Florence: Santo Spirito, Nave. Brunelleschi's interior, with its strict canonical lines and 'ideal' semi-circular arches over antique columns and high coussinets, is considered a classical development of Early Renaissance architecture.

14

modest secondary position as far as municipal function and representational pretensions are concerned.

Within the wider context of European city life at the end of the Middle Ages the Vecchio Tower, together with the self-effacing Bargello Tower, appears in all its unique political significance. Now that the aristocratic *società degli torri,* with its eighty and more towers, has been destroyed, the city outline stresses the single, dominating tower of the communal palace which deputises for all the other towers, dismantled in the end, and stands as the symbol of a new political era. This applies also to the tower of the Town Hall in Siena (which exceeds Florence's in height, and for reasons of rivalry *had* to surpass it), as well as to other Italian communal palaces.

It was in this final but still medieval guise of aristocratic fortress that the pride of the 'new' middle classes created for itself in Florence a symbol whose undoubted tension and elegance, against the general background, represents

15

15 Florence: San Marco Monastery: View of the Cloisters. The original Sylvestrine Monastery was transferred in 1436 to the Dominicans of Fiesole, who between 1437 and 1452, under Michelozzo's direction, restored the complex, which had fallen into ruin. Michelozzo also created the cloisters, a charming mixture of Gothic and Early Renaissance styles, full of genuinely inspired feeling. San Marco is famed for its frescoes (Plates 29 to 31) by Fra Angelico who worked here from 1435/1436 until 1445; and also for the fact that Savonarola did his preaching here against the world's frivolity, and proclaimed his 'Heavenly Kingdom on earth'. It was from San Marco too that he was led out to the stake.

16. Florence: Palazzo Vecchio (also called Palazzo della Signoria). The Palace was built between 1298 and 1314, probably from plans by Arnolfo di Cambio. Originally, as a symbol of civic pride at a time of growing municipal power, it was called 'Palazzo dei Priori' (seat of the Masters of the Guilds, and of the Republic's Supreme Council), and also 'Palazzo del Popolo', because the old Florentine Republic was a democracy. Before he was banished, Dante frequented it for a brief period as one of the 'Priors'. Walter von Brienne, the Usurper, also resided here under the name of 'Duke of Athens' until he was ignominiously expelled. Michelozzi added to its facilities by installing an emergency water-tank in the attics, and more convenient stairs (1446). In Cosimo the Elder's time the seat of government was temporarily transferred to the Medici Palace. Duke Alessandro brought the Parliament back to the 'Old Palace', and Cosimo I then governed permanently there from 1537 onwards. The Palazzo della Signoria was now called 'Palazzo Ducale' (the Ducal Palace). When the Medici Residence was once more transferred to the Pitti Palace, the building finally became the 'Palazzo Vecchio' or 'Old Palace', and from then on had only a representational function. The Tower contained a small 'exclusive' prison for particularly dangerous political offenders. The 'Pater Patriae' Cosimo de Medici and the zealous monk Savonarola were held there for a time.

new, upward-striving art trends which stand in indissoluble conflict with a serious and pathetic rhetoric, a vocabulary of swallow-tailed and rectangular battlements, tower defences and squared stone bosses which still belongs to the Middle Ages. Jacob Burckhardt summed up the essential features of this structure with laconic precision in his 'Cicerone', using only seventeen words: 'Greatness, memories, stone-colour, and fantastic tower-structure confer on this building a value which far surpasses the artistic.'

Florence's economic, political and cultural upsurge around 1300 can be read of course not only in its secular architecture but particularly in the ecclesiastical buildings. This was the time when the great churches that still grace the city came into being in quick succession. With them the Middle Ages reached its zenith in great and simple form. Santa Maria Novella was begun

17 Florence, Palazzo Vecchio: The Courtyard. The late medieval architecture of the courtyard was converted to pre-Rennaissance by Michelozzo in 1453. In 1565 the arcades were decorated by frescoes designed by Giorgio Vasari. The most important features of his design are the 18 views of cities of the Habsburg empire (out of reverence for the Austrian bride of the Archduke Ferdinand, as the courtyard was decorated especially for his wedding). Verrocchio's very attractive "Putto with Fish" stands in the middle of the courtyard, in the centre of the fountain, and is an allegory of the 'Socratic Eros', originally created for the Medici villa in Careggi.

18 Florence, Palazzo Vecchio: Sala dell'Udienza (Audience Chamber). One of the ancient staterooms of the Florentine Republic. The portal was created by Benedetto da Maiano (1529). The frescoes, amongst the finest of Italian Mannirism, are the work of Francesco Salviati (approximately 1550/60) and depict the history of the Roman consular tribune and commander Furius Cammillus, who conquered several Italian tribes and occupied Veji in the 4th century B.C.

18

in 1246 (Plate 9), but it was to take two hundred years before the great Renaissance architect Leon Battista Alberti could complete it. Santa Croce began to expand from 1295 on (Plates 10 and 11) to become one of Italy's greatest and most distinguished Franciscan churches, founded according to legend by St. Francis himself (1181–1226) in 1209, and just six hundred years later (1857–1863) was given a somewhat stiff marble façade, in the form of a pseudo-historical incrustation style, though the façade fits well enough into the city scene and corresponds to the general style. This now stands before the majestically simple Church of the Mendicant Friars, a splendid yet touching tribute by the Florentines of to-day to their medieval past. Tradition has it that Arnolfo di Cambio, Master of the Palazzo Vecchio, was the leading architect here too. He is also accepted as the spirit behind the new structure of the city's largest church, the Cathedral of Santa Maria del Fiore (Plates 5 to 8). This church with its fabulous and costly external garb of incrusted white and dark marble panels forms an unmistakeable and much-praised ensemble together with the Campanile and the Baptistery.

Arnolfo di Cambio did not live to see the completion of his great work, hardly more indeed than part of the brickwork, for he died as early as 1301, just five years after the laying of the foundation-stone. The structure remained as it was and was then carried further in two stages, in 1331 and under Talenti from 1357 on. In the succeeding period it attracted two of the most outstanding artists in Florence: Giotto, who tackled the Campanile from 1334 onwards, and Brunelleschi, who completed the Dome one hundred and fifty years after the beginning of the whole undertaking (1434–1461), this being what we must regard as the beginning of the Renaissance in Italian architectural history. In this case too, the façade met with misfortune. It remained unfinished, was torn down in 1588 as a result of architectural damage, and was not rebuilt until the end of the nineteenth century, with fair historical adaptation to the original facework of choir and nave.

In discussing the contribution made by the city to Italian Gothic, illustrated in this volume by three examples that at the same time represent three different religious architectural requirements—the Parish Church (Santa Maria Novella), the Church of the Mendicant Friars or the Monastery (Santa Croce) and the Cathedral or Bishop's Church (Cathedral of Santa Maria del Fiore)—we touch on a theme which has long been the subject of controversy in the history of art and culture. Jacob Buckhardt, writing in 1855, regarded everything Gothic as a basically foreign and problematic phenomenon on classical Italian soil. 'The intrusion of Gothic architectural forms from the North was fateful for Italian art, a misfortune if you like, but

only for the unskilled, who would not in any case have been in a position to help themselves' *(Cicerone)*. Only the newer way of regarding art made it possible for justice to be done to this style, as a special form, the Italian version of 'Latin Gothic'. In coming to terms with the gothic of French cathedrals some specific Italian features, found throughout Italian art, were developed, such as a pleasing awareness of space, a way of thinking in terms of vast, harmoniously laid out and clearly separated spatial units. This

19 Florence: Bargello: The Courtyard. The Bargello, originally the 'Palazzo del Podestà', or seat of the Mayor, was built in 1255 as a token of victory over the aristocracy. The father of Arnolfo di Cambio, builder of the Cathedral, is said to have been the architect. An older family tower, one of the Torri *of the noble families, was fitted into the structure, symbolising the aspirations to power of the 'new' middle class. To-day the tower is one of Florence's landmarks. That haughty architecture has witnessed significant scenes in Florentine history. The Pazzi conspirators, for instance, were cruelly tortured to death in the Bargello's dark cells (1478). Previously, on the outer walls, Castagno had portrayed, in mockery and ridicule, the hanging of the Albizzi conspirators. Later on Botticelli carried out a similar commission depicting the Pazzi conspirators on the grim walls. At that time the Palace was the seat of legal authority (Bargello), hence the name to-day. The building now contains one of the most important collections of sculpture, mostly from the Uffizi, which in the nineteenth century was no longer able to house its vast collection of works of art.*

characteristic, which was later to leave its imprint even on Renaissance architecture, had already found expression in Italian gothic.

One sociological and political circumstance stands out as even more important than these questions of scholarly assessment and interpretation, which inhibit rather than enrich the visual experience for the untrained visitor. Just as happened with the construction of the Palazzo Vecchio, the rebuilding of the Cathedral was also from the very first a political issue of the greatest importance, and a matter on which every Florentine, from the humblest workman to the lofty Rector of a Guild or a Town Councillor, took sides in the liveliest fashion, not forgetting the polemics. Florence can now be comprehended as an art metropolis *in toto*, one where every significant undertaking is backed by the majority of the citizens, united in their desire for art and creativity, and one in which in certain situations the entire creative strength of the city can concentrate on a single task. Innumerable meetings of City Council and Commission took place on the subject; juries were made up and again dissolved, under protest, as being biased; many people died broken-hearted at the building's failure; old friendships broke up; families fell out for decades because of differences over aesthetic matters, something as unusual and unheard-of then as it would be now.

After Arnolfo di Cambio's early death an open competition was announced, at the third construction stage under Talenti, in which every Florentine could take part, independently of status or profession. This procedure was repeated for every single part and section of the structure. Soon a Talenti and an Orcagna party formed which waged a campaign against each other as venomously as Ghibelline and Guelph had once done. The ground-plan finally accepted in 1366 had been worked out by a committee of no less than thirteen master architects and 11 painters. Eight other master architects signed as responsible for the elevation. The older models were thereupon publicly destroyed. Many of the minutes of the Commission sessions have been preserved, and there seem to have been some pretty hectic scenes as the rival groups around Talenti, Orcagna, Taddeo Gaddi and Neri di Fioravante vied with each other in speaking out of turn.

It remains a miracle and a tribute to the artistic sense and great integrating talent of the Florentine people, in everything pertaining to art and culture, that the work was not spoiled in the end by too many 'cooks' but seems to to-day's observer to have been cast in one mould.

The Age of Giotto and Dante

The creative forces of the city itself were hardly adequate to carry on the manifold artistic tasks facing it: a local School was just beginning to be formed. At the commencement of the great period of Florentine art, therefore, outside artists were 'imported', a procedure that was repeated also in Rome. Later the reverse would be the case and the whole of Italy would for a while become 'Florentine'; the Mediterranean area with France, Spain and even Hungary (Masolino 1427) would talk the language of Florence in matters of art and culture; artists from Northern Europe, German and Flemish in the main, would make a pilgrimage to Florence as if it were Mecca; native artists would become the favoured 'export items' from the city on the Arno. For the moment, however, it was outside forces that were relied upon or, according to the political conception of the day, 'foreigners'. Venetian specialists, trained in the then purely Greek-Byzantine style native to the lagoon city, and familiar with the highly-developed handling there of glass, paste and glass-cutting (Murano), created a considerable part of the roof mosaic on the Baptistery. Arnolfo di Cambio too came from outside, from Colle di Val d'Elsa. Duccio, who painted the famous altar painting in the Rucellai Chapel in Santa Maria Novella (about 1285) was summoned from Siena, to the great annoyance of his fellow-countrymen. Even the great Giotto (1266–1336) was not born within the city walls but in a tiny corner of the country of the Florentine Contado, in Colle di Vespignano. It is not even certain that Cimabue (1240 to after 1302), honoured by Dante as the 'Father of Florentine Painting', was born and brought up in Florence. He is mentioned for the first time in Rome in 1272, was active in Pisa and Assisi, but only in passing in Florence.

With Giotto a new chapter opens in the art history not only of Florence or Italy but of Europe. Giotto is represented in this volume by the celebrated fresco portraying the Death of St. Francis, from the legend of St. Francis in the Capella Bardi in the Franciscan Church of Santa Croce (Plate 27), a moving late work full of classical restraints and lofty spirituality, to which Winckelmann's phrase about 'noble simplicity, silent greatness' applies just as much as to any important important Greek or Roman classic. The argument that the Renaissance began here and not one hundred years later, once the Soft Style, 'international Gothic' *(Gotico internazionale)*, had been superseded, cannot be dismissed out of hand.

Giotto is honoured in a famous Florentine document dating from 1334, as a Master of high *scientia et doctrina,* not simply as a man of vision and a creative artist but as a man of outstanding 'wisdom and learning', though this may only be a standard expression then applied to all important artists. One hundred years later, in his *'Memoirs'* dating from the mid-fifteenth century, Lorenzo Ghiberti ventured a precise art-historical assessment and classification, connecting the revival of art in the modern sense with the names of Cimabue and above all Giotto. He also related the famous story which, via Vasari, has come down to our own day, of how Giotto as a boy was guarding the sheep near his home village of Vespignano and drawing one member of the flock when he was surprised by Cimabue who, coming along the highway from Bologna and struck as if by something miraculous, at once recognized the youth's extraordinary talent.

In choice of subject as well as in presentation Giotto broke completely with the medieval Byzantine style, the *maniera greca,* which before his time had dominated Italian religious painting virtually to the exclusion of other styles. Suddenly we find ourselves looking at living, breathing people; not 'mummified forms' as Jacob Burckhardt so aptly and cuttingly describes them, but people of flesh and blood, with a definable personality and psyche, an earthly material quality and three-dimensionality, people who could literally cast a shadow—this applied even when saints were portrayed. Later this was to become one of Masaccio's main themes, as in his painting of the Lame Man being healed when St. Peter's shadow falls on him (Florence, Church of Santa Maria del Carmine, Brancacci Chapel, after 1423).

Giotto builds up his compositions on the basis of the human figure alone. All his pictorial inventiveness originates in his portrayals of human beings and his entire *oeuvre* concentrates on depicting basic human situations. The formal technique that was so important in the *maniera greca,* such as the hieratic gold priming, the lavish clouds, the stylized architectonic and landscape scenes, which look like stage sets, schemes based on framework and decorations designed to fill the picture surface, plus costly, mannered work on drapery and folds, are reduced with him to a minimum, or become merely a side issue, or are even rejected completely. He felt that they distracted him from the central theme that he followed throughout his life as if possessed—as indeed the only two artists to match him in stature, Masaccio in the fifteenth century and Michelangelo in the sixteenth, were also possessed. He was constantly preoccupied with representing inner processes as expressed in concrete terms in gestures and expressive bearing. These can now be observed for the first time in living people, Tuscan contemporaries, and are not slavishly copied from a long Byzantine pictorial tradition that had now been exhausted.

Giotto's work is invariably clear-cut and great; every new picture is a new discovery; every painting a human drama. And from his total *oeuvre* a new artistic language emerges, in content as well as in form. Above all, Giotto freed painting from the domination of 'Greek' colour, which had originally been strident, even gaudy, but in its decadent phase became increasingly flat

20

20 Florence: Medici-Riccardi Palace. This building, created by Michelozzo from 1444 onwards, is the prelude to Early Renaissance palace architecture in Florence and up until 1540 was the seat of the Head of the Medici family. Later it became the private residence of their wives, widows and children. The former brilliant furnishings, apart from a small remnant (Medici Chapel with the painting by Benozzo Gozzoli), disappeared when Piero de' Medici was banished.

21

21 Florence: Medici-Riccardi Palace. The Courtyard. The Courtyard, with its refined and well-articulated architecture, deliberately contrasting with the robust, defensive exterior, is one of the most elegant creations of the Early Renaissance in Florence.

and dull. He operates with a few easily distinguished basic colours, which stand out in his frescoes in light and bright transparency, their tonal and lighting values shaded off in ultramarines, and brought into a harmonious unity without any 'forcing', for in Florence feeling for the individual value and character of every colour and every pigment was retained up to the end of the Renaissance. The typical Florentine attitude to colour can be seen already in Giotto. 'The colours stand out with great precision, firm, resonant, bright and effective, ready to enter into combat with one another and become reconciled in a higher unity' (Th. Hetzer: *Giotto*. Frankfurt am Main, n.d.).

Like Dante's work, Giotto's *Oeuvre* was an erratic boulder standing out in its time like a monument impossible to overlook, one that so towered into the era following that no art was possible directly afterwards which did not take it into account or produce successors. Like Dante, he had the effect of creating a large number of schools than ever before and his followers are legion: Stefano Fiorentino, Taddeo Gaddi, Puccio Capanna, Giottino, Bernardo Daddi, Maso da Banco, Andrea da Firenze, to name but a few of the most important of the 'Giottists' in the fourteenth century. Like Dante too, Giotto's fate was to have the art of his followers succumb to mere imitation, exhaust itself in more and more anaemic repetition, until it ran out in the sand and became banal. Just as Dante's linguistic rhythm and music, his ingenious metre and the world of his poetic images ultimately sank among those who plagiarized him to the level of utter travesty, occasional lyrics, political and polemical satire, and propaganda or erotically obscene song-writing, so Giotto's discoveries were carried further into flatter and flatter patterns, to such an extent that by 1400 all that was left in Assisi, Padua or Florence was pale derivatives of Giotto's epoch-making productions.

For this decline, however, Giotto is no more responsible than Dante for his more trivial followers. Little can be added to Burckhardt's judgement that: 'Giotto himself produced a stream of discoveries and new creations. Perhaps no other painter than he has so fully reconstituted art and set it off in a new direction after him' *(Cicerone)*.

To treat of Giotto and Florence is also to treat of Dante. His contribution to Italian national poetry may be considered greater even than Giotto's, Masaccio's, or Michelangelo's to Italian art. Giotto's figures have often been said to be personifications of Dante's. Dante's visions on the other hand could well be scenes for Giotto's figures. Giotto and Dante can only be seen here as a 'unity of opposites'. Temperamentally and spiritually they were fundamentally different, comparable only in their artistic intensity, and yet they were rooted in the same Florentine soil out of which their art grew. In terms of Schiller's categories, Giotto should be classified as 'naive' and Dante as 'sentimental', the one creating out of secure artistic instincts, natural humanity, naive psychology and observation felt rather than considered; and the other always substituting for his poetic features the acuity of Florentine rationalism, and the intellectual approach typical of Florence.

To that extent Dante—as a humanist, man of letters, poetic theorist, political scientist and social Utopian—possessed all the characteristics of the ideal *uomo universale,* the universal genius, as it emerged in Florence one hundred and fifty years later, at the beginning of the Renaissance. As an innovator he challenged a whole cultural epoch: on one side the dry monotony of the decaying world of medieval schools of theology and scholasticism, its teaching become dry as dust through constant repetition, analysis and interpretations of interpretations; and on the other, the world of chivalry and the *Minne,* the lyrics of the Provençal troubadours, frozen into mannerisms.

The political and social scene in Florence around 1250 was opposed to Dante's spirit of renewal. It was an extraordinarily politicised situation, in which all values were being called in question. The aristocracy had played out its historic role and for the first time the 'people', in the form of broad strata of the population, were entering the political arena. The *popolo grasso (grosso),* the guilds and middle class were pressing forward. The constant family feuds

22

Previous page:
22 Florence: Pitti Palace. The Palace was begun by the Pitti family only a few years after the Medici Palace, and certainly in clearly-stated competition with that of Luca Fancelli (1457–1466). In 1550 it was purchased by the Medici. Up to the eighteenth and nineteenth centuries it was continually being altered and finally was enlarged to gigantic size. When Florence was provisionally Italy's capital (1864–1865), King Victor Emmanuel II had his residence on the upper floor. To-day it is a museum containing many of the main Medici items which even after the building of the Uffizi were privately held by the family.

23 Florence: Pitti Palace. Detail of Façade.

24 Florence: Strozzi Palace. This Palace, begun in 1485 by the Florentine merchant and humanist Filippo di Matteo Strozzi and completed about 1500 with the active assistance of the Medici for local architectural reasons, is the latest in our series and also the loveliest. In it the lofty theme of rustication, with deeply chanelled joints between the masonry blocks, is carried out in the most consistent manner. Enthusiastic expressions of appreciation have been forthcoming about this 'Miracle of rustication.' 'Every stone has the effect of a swelling muscle. The wall rises elastically and full of inner strength, up from the bottom, almost by itself' (G. Kauffmann, 1962).

24

and the party struggles between aristocracy, commercially-minded patricians, guilds and lower levels of the population had its counterpart in the cultural field, in the form of great spiritual unrest. The stylized traditions of the old *trouvère* poetry of love lyrics, and the theologians' philosophical problems, ossified in symbolism, no longer sufficed to express this unrest. Both troubadours and theologians did of course deal with the central themes of love, desire, death and pain. But against these Dante set the spiritual power of the 'creative Eros'. New values were thus brought into being. Love for the adored, idealized and therefore distant and unattainable lady was the expression of the new 'nobility of soul', which was demonstrated precisely by the fact that the far-off beloved could only be honoured and sung, not physically desired. To Dante's generation feminine beauty appeared to be a reflection of celestial perfection, and the beloved the personification of heavenly wisdom and of a divine plan of creation manifesting itself in rare cases in the form of a physically and spiritually perfect woman. The adored one became stylized as an angelic intercessor between God and the world. In accord with this angelic aspect, no sooner had Dante's Beatrice and Petrarch's Laura passed from childhood to puberty than they were elevated by the Florentine poets to the rank of sources of inspiration, angelic child-women, untouched and untouchable. The early, far too early death of the childlike beloved (Beatrice, or Laura) was experienced in a mystical sense as a tragic act of purification. She became in the kingdom of poetic imagination the immortal beloved. Her virginity also now acquired a plausible biographical context. Or can we fancy Laura or Beatrice as fulsome matrons, with an indolent Florentine shopkeeper for a husband, and a host of children tugging at their skirts?

The cult of feminine and virginal beauty provided a concrete basis for Aristotle's rediscovered aesthetics and made them Christian. Thus the artistic cult of the Madonna throughout the entire Renaissance and Baroque periods was now philosophically and psychologically prepared. The outward form of this poetic devotion was the *dolce stil nuovo,* the 'new sweet style', a vernacular literature based on the Tuscan-Florentine dialect. The knightly Courts of Love were replaced by metropolitan 'Love Courts'. 'It was a highly-charged, intellectually-lively atmosphere, attracting the fairest women in the city—Dante counted sixty of them in Florence—a divine Court in the centre of which stood Beatrice, Selvaggia, Monna Lagia, Monna Vanna and others. Their outward appearance, dress, passing mood, friendships and family all played a part in their glorification, while the city itself provided the theatre on which was played out the drama of the anguish and joy of love, poetically transfigured (L. Olschki, 1958).

Employing poetic insight, Dante—like Giotto—triumphed over a narrow world that was still basically provincial, and spiritualized a limited earthly reality. His language was the Italian of the people, which he called upon in the struggle against the dry and enervated Latin of the church. It was this language, no longer privileged and identified with certain social strata (only the clergy and a few educated people understood Latin) but understood by everyone, that laid the foundation for a new national literary language and speech which is still to-day the determinant of Italian culture. Dante found in Italy, which had been completely decentralized after the Graeco-Roman period, no less than fourteen established and sometimes very different dialects. In his treatise 'De Vulgari Eloquentia' ('Concerning Popular Rhetoric') he cleverly set out the reasons why it was Florentine that he had selected as the framework of his new literary language. This was because, of all the Italian dialects, it was closest to Latin and—according to Olschki—to the 'solemn majesty of literary Latin' of the Classical Period (not therefore of the Middle and Church Latin decadence).

All classes were seized by enthusiasm for the new vernacular poetry. Worship of Dante began even in his lifetime and persists to-day. There is hardly a single Italian who cannot recite at least a few lines of Dante by heart, and this does not apply only to the so-called educated classes. Visitors to Italy

25 Florence: The Strozzi Palace. The Courtyard architecture of the Strozzi Palace is by Cronaca (after 1497) and matches in quality Michelozzi's courtyard in the Medici-Riccardi Palace. (Plate 21).

Pages 44 and 45:
26 Florence: Ponte Vecchio and view up the river towards the Piazzale Michelangelo. Florence's oldest bridge, one of the most famous and remarkable in the world, stands on the site of a Roman building on the old Via Cassia, which cut through the Roman Florentia. The first medieval bridge was made of timber. The first stone bridge came in 1080; the second, following a collapse, in 1170; and the third in 1333, after the great 'Flood', the worst in Florence's history, more devastating even than the 1963 catastrophe. The shops on the bridge have been in existence since the thirteenth century and were originally State property, rented out for high sums as one of the best and busiest commercial sites in old Florence. Not until 1495 were these botteghe *sold to private individuals. In 1593 Archduke Ferdinando I decreed that henceforth only goldsmiths would be allowed to establish themselves on the bridge. The crowning connecting passage which allowed the Medici to ply speedily between their administration headquarters in the Uffizi and the new family residence in the Pitti Palace unhindered by public traffic dates from the time of Vasari (about 1570). The houses at the bridgeheads on the right and left banks of the Arno are historically skilful adaptations replacing those blown up in August 1944 to form tank barriers, thus saving the Ponte Vecchio itself.*

25

are constantly astonished when the vegetable-seller in Verona's marketplace, or the pizza-baker in Trastevere, suddenly declaims Dante's classical and sonorous verses. There is always some excuse for doing so because Dante's works, like Goethe's, have taken root in the popular mind in the form of a series of quotations. Central to all of Dante's writings is the classical identification of beauty and morality. He thus gave the most resolute expression to an ideal which has never lost its validity, even in the Italy of to-day. Beauty as a virtue in itself has always been one of the fundamental tenets of that essentially aesthetically-minded people, who put it into practice every day in the art of setting the table in the simplest of country inns; in the modest lay-out of the fruit-dealer in the street; or the way in which the azaleas are arranged in stalls on the Spanish Steps in Rome. Such examples combine to make the Italians loved by other Europeans, whose affection is always ensured even though the politics of the day in Italy or the frequently chaotic-seeming business life may not always meet the conception others have of orderly behaviour. When all is said and done, every political action and every demonstration of political will in Italy is observed and judged from the artistic and aesthetic aspect. A politician without the gift of the gab or persuasive rhetoric will never amount to very much here. Socialist and communist parades invariably became aesthetic ventures in this country, with forests of red flags billowing in the breeze, which is how Bertolucci depicted them in his film *1900*. This was the feeling that in perverted form played itself out among the Italian Futurists, as shown in their manifesto on Mussolini's colonial war in Abyssinia, when they demanded 'aesthetic war' and—with Marinetti—lauded the 'fiery orchids of the mitrailleuse' (an ancestor of the machine-gun); the 'new architecture of big tanks; geometric air-squadrons; and spirals of smoke from burning villages.'

The same compulsion to render every aspect of life aesthetic can be seen in the Renaissance theory of the State, which translated the cult of the beautiful into political terms, conceived of the State as a work of art, and compared social reconstruction to a beautiful and perfect piece of architecture.

Thoughts such as these must have been in Dante's mind when in his treatise 'De Monarchia' he dreamt of general peace being the indispensable prerequisite for human welfare in society. A universal ruler of imperial rank with great moral authority seemed to him to be the guarantee of 'eternal peace'. In Dante's view, however, the new morality need not necessarily be based on Christian theology, but could be thought of as grounded in Aristotelian ethics, another anticipation of the Renaissance.

Dante was unable to identify wholly with either Pope or Emperor, since that would have been in contradiction with his Utopian concept of reconciliation. Neither a whole-hearted Ghibelline nor a committed Guelph, he was reckoned by his contemporaries in Florence to be among the 'Whites', i.e. 'Ghibelline' Guelphs. At that time the old parties, Guelphs and 'Imperials', were so mixed up that there was scarcely any difference between 'left' Ghibellines and 'right' Papists. The paradox becomes clear when we discover from Florence's records that Dante, himself of aristocratic lineage, was compelled for party reasons not only to condemn his fellow-poet and social equal the aristocratic Guido Cavalcante, but to take him the verdict in his *Torre* (now part of the modern Villa Bellosguardo). This must have hit Dante particularly hard, since Cavalcante was a friend of his and he had more than once praised his poetic achievement. This contradictory attitude—liberal we might call it to-day—paid off badly for Dante, who always found himself between two stools in the quarrelsome political scene of the time. As a 'white' Guelph he was one of the Priors of Florence in 1300. In 1301 his liberal group lost power to the radical 'black' Guelphs, and Dante had to leave the territory. As we have seen, he was sentenced to death in his absence. Never again did he visit the city. For him it became a part of a poetic super-reality, attainable and tangible only in his poetic imagination, like the early deceased, beloved Beatrice. He consequently declined a humiliating amnesty in 1316 which would have allowed him to return only under conditions that were unacceptable. His ambivalent feelings for his home town found shattering expression in a strongly-worded challenge to Emperor Henry VII, during the latter's visit to Italy for the purpose of reconstituting the Hohenstaufen Empire, to lay Florence low and efface the memory of it from history forever. He had nothing now in common with the city where he had been baptised and where he had hoped, as the crowning-point of his life, to be made 'Poeta laureatus'.

In his restless wanderings through northern Italy he found consolation in studying the ancient writers and ancient philosophy, especially the fatalistic Stoics. He had begun this return to the *sapienta veterum* (Wisdom of the Ancients) in 1292, after the death of Beatrice Portinari. It was an attitude fully in keeping with the spiritual milieu. Free discussion groups were set up everywhere to deal with political and moral problems and were supported by the provincial aristocracy and educated middle class. In these circles of *filosofanti,* as Dante called them, the educational traditions of the ancient world and the intellectual liberalism of the great Emperor Frederick II were carried on, and a foundation laid for fifteenth and sixteenth century Florentine academicism. These were secular forms of the medieval, clerical 'Disputations', and the outcome of the debates between intelligent men affected the entire city as much as the results of the planning competitions for the Cathedral, the Campanile or the Palazzo Vecchio. Florence always had a penchant for settling controversial points of view by talking them over. Dante's *'Vita Nuova'* (begun in 1293), the story of his love, is one result of this training. In the *'Convivio'* (1306–1309) Dante described the history of his intellectual education. The works that followed were always autobiographical in tendency, even the *'Divina Commedia',* which occupied the remainder of his life from 1307 on. This describes the poet's enlightened ascent to God and is a poetical account of the fantastic path which led the poet 'through all heavens and hells', out of the spiritual slavery of the medieval world into a 'Kingdom of Freedom' and the spirit, which is the beginning of the modern world. In the strictest symmetry, constructed, as it were, according to the precise rules of architecture, Dante summed up his view of the world in one hundred songs, including the various stages of purification: Hell *(Inferno),* Purgatory *(Purgatorio)* and Heaven *(Paradiso).* The Utopian content of the poem, with the vestiges of medieval piety and attraction to the future life that it contains, seem out of date now, insignificant and anachronistic. But the 'wealth and power of Dante's poetry' (L. Olschki 1958) have lived on, together with his language and his unmistakably harmonious style, his innovatory metaphors and his universal aspirations. Like Goethe's *Faust* some hundreds of years later, Dante's *Commedia* gives full expression in a profusion of visions and images to the learning of the period, to its collective consciousness, its dreams and disappointments, its hopes and fears, its splendour and its failure, its passions and its capacity for grief.

Like Giotto's work, Dante's poetry was the determining factor, at least as far as form and style are concerned, of the period that followed, the whole of the fourteenth century and the early fifteenth—a period that was once again marked in Florence by harsh social problems and upheavals in the structure of society.

Humanism and the Renaissance
The Emergence of a National Style in Florence

Renaissance—*rinascita*—rebirth, a rebirth of the arts, the birth of a new culture born out of the old. At the very height of this period Giorgio Vasari, its most famous chronicler, who came from Arezzo, had already recognized what the change meant. His *Lives,* the 'Biographies of the most excellent Painters, Sculptors and Architects' of his day, first appeared in 1550 and classifies it accurately on the whole, labelling it as 'classical'. This label is still

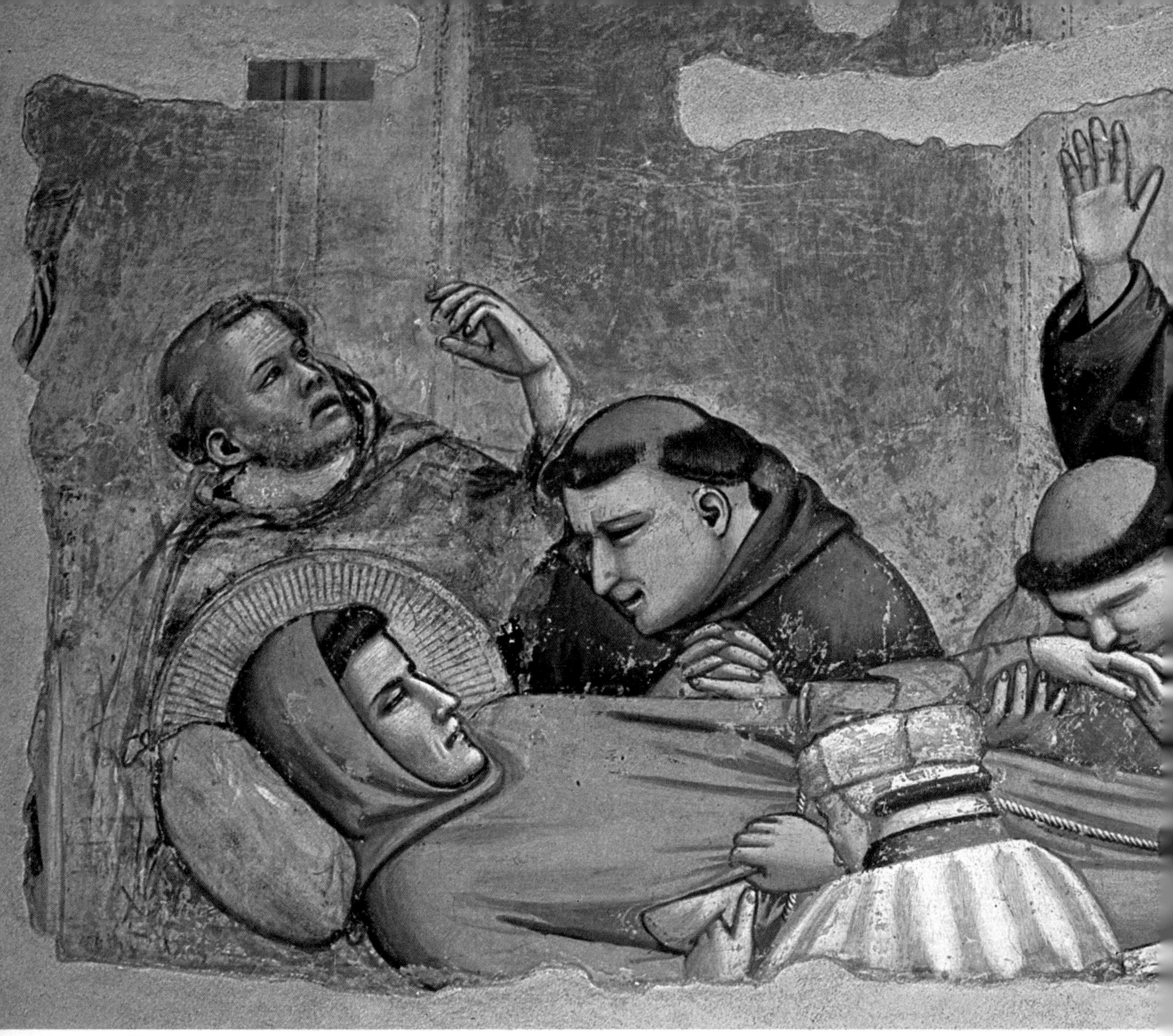

27

27 Giotto: 'The Death of St. Francis', circa *1320. Florence, Santa Croce. The fresco in the Capella Bardi is one of Giotto's late works and illustrates the great artistic breakthrough in Dante's time.*

accepted by art historians without question today; Vasari's conception of history has indeed remained valid over four hundred years of art-historical research. Since 1850 it has merely been improved and amplified, beginning with Jacob Burkhardt's basic work on the Italian Renaissance. And the accepted concept that the entire art and culture of Europe after Christ should really be seen as a series of Renaissance and resumptions, 'renovations' (even in the Middle Ages), and that the Renaissance in the fifteenth and sixteenth centuries in Italy was merely the most consistent and successful and has operated up to our own time.

In stating above, in connection with Giotto and Dante, that the 'Rebirth of the arts' and the development of a national Italian style coincide, and that the turning-point can be fixed as early as 1250, we have the authority of Vasari as witness. He was the first to divide the art of the known world at the time into three great eras: the brilliant classical period in Athens and Rome; a 'dark' transitional period of decline, decay and cultural barbarism (or, in our terms, the whole of the Middle Ages); and finally the period of 'rebirth', the *'rinascita'* of the classical spirit which he places at circa 1250, half a generation

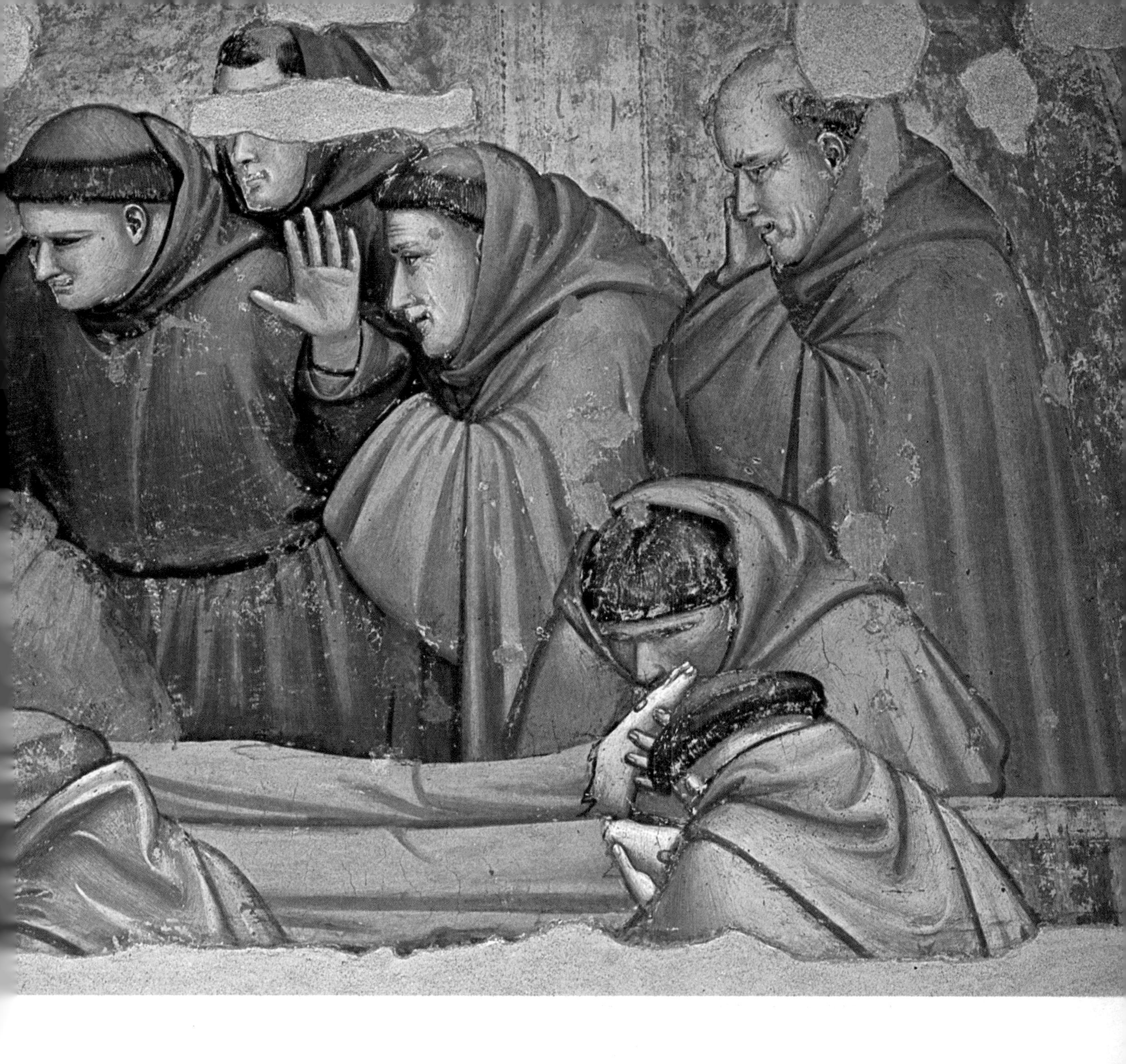

before the birth of Dante and Giotto.

The feeling that a turning-point had been reached must have been in the air in Tuscany. Circa 1280 an important find of ancient shards was made in Arezzo, an old centre of Etruscan-Tuscan and later of Roman culture. This was nothing out of the ordinary on Italian soil, which was full of such discoveries and still is, so much so that almost every deep digging yields such treasures, and indeed uncovered the whole Middle Ages. What was unusual and new was the reaction of cultured circles in Arezzo. A commission was formed, consisting of draughtsmen, sculptors and art-minded citizens, which called for a report on the findings by the historian Ristoro d'Arezzo. This was concluded in 1282. Giotto and Dante were then youths of sixteen or seventeen. Ristoro's report clearly indicates the delight of the 'connoisseurs', who dated the discovery approximately correctly in stating that the fragments had been in the earth for over a thousand years. 'When they saw them, they were beside themselves with delight, reached a pitch of excitement so to speak, raised a loud clamour and remained thunderstruck . . . They were amazed that human nature could show such subtlety and artistic skill . . .

[They said] these artists must have been divine, or the vases must have fallen from heaven, for they could not understand how they could have been made so [perfect] in that shape and colour as works of art.' In their time the 1282 discovery and report merely represented an anticipatory procedure and demonstrated nothing but a general trend and willingness. Humanism, and a direct return to the ancient world was still primarily a literary and philosophical phenomenon. Medieval tradition in form and content, and 'International' Court Gothic, were still all-powerful and largely determined the art production of the late thirteenth and the whole of the fourteenth century. Three dates mark the beginning of the 'rebirth', and the triumph of the new trend in art. They define at the same time the period generally referred to as the Early Renaissance. The Platonic Academy was founded in Florence about 1440, within the circle of Cosimo 'the Elder' Medici and at his instigation. Greek scholars such as Manuel Chrysoloras and Bessarion were coming to Italy at the beginning of the century from Byzantium, which was becoming increasingly unsafe as a 'bastion of Europe'. That city had come into direct cultural contact with Italy through the capture of Constantinople in the year 1204, and as early as 1400 émigrés had founded special circles for the study of Classical Greek, and were instituting a Plato renaissance.

The last Christian divine service was held in Hagia Sophia in Constantinople in May 1453, a scene movingly described by Stefan Zweig in his book *The Tide of Fortune*. The city finally fell to the Turks on May 29, 1453 and the church of St. Sophia was turned into a mosque, thus closing a chapter of world history. A second wave of migration thereafter led further Greek-Byzantine scholars to Italy, especially to Florence, and the ancient Greek legacy which had survived in the Byzantine Empire was now looked after in Italy. In the corridors of Hagia Sophia on the other hand the various Greek readings of the New Testament were no longer discussed, nor the question of how far Platonic philosophy had prepared the way for Christian doctrine. Henceforth, in one of Christendom's proudest monuments, it was the Koran which would be read and interpreted.

In 1492, following a sixty-one-day voyage, Columbus landed at Guanahani in what is to-day San Salvador, and afterwards discovered Cuba and Haiti. This was a year that signified a great turning-point in history. Europe's centre of gravity was shifted more and more to the West. A political and cultural front was being built up against the Turkish-Moslem East. The 'Turkish menace' was to be a constant political factor in determining European policy for two hundred and thirty years, until the defeat of the Osman soldiery in 1683, before the gates of Vienna. The sway of Islam over large sections of what had long been known as the 'Old world', and over the whole of the ancient Orient, had its parallel in the Christianization of the 'New World' in the West, first Central America and then the Northern areas of South America. It was then that the 'Europeanization' of the world began, for the world was still 'Eurocentric' by inclination. It was significant that in the same year, 1492, and in close association with Columbus' expedition, the last Arab rump of Empire in Spain, the stronghold of Granada, went ingloriously under. The Moors, literally driven into the sea, had to withdraw to the North African shores of the Barbary Coast, where the chief towns, Melilla and Oran, were also ultimately taken by the Castilians in 1497 and 1509. The end of the Spanish *Reconquista*, or Reconquest, was thus at the same time the beginning of the Spanish and Portuguese Conquest of America. A world had been discovered, and the result was a new feeling about the world, and a new view of the world.

From this aspect, Jacob Burckhardt's formula according to which the Italian Renaissance is the 'discovery of the world and of Man' acquires a universal political background that points far beyond purely cultural history. The source of the new Humanist and Renaissance movement lay in Florence. It was there that the cultural superstructure was created for the political about-turn. Florence's importance in world history lay in the fact that the new style and way of thinking soon acquired an 'international' i.e. an all-

28 Masaccio: 'Trinita' (Trinity), detail: approximately 1425. Florence. Santa Maria Novella. This mural marks the beginning of Early Rennaissance painting. The new 'classical' style is evident in the usage of the discoveries of perspective by the great Brunelleschi, the classic architectural framework, the symmetry and monumentality in the composition and the depiction of individual characters and their inner feelings. This work was of great importance for the young Leonardo and Michelangelo and it was revered and diligently studied during the High-Rennaissance.

30

29, 30 Fra Angelico: the 'Angel of the Annunciation', and 'Mary' (Details). Florence, Monastery of San Marco. These frescoes, created by Brother Fra Angelico for his mother-house in the forties of the fifteenth century, typify the formal language of 'Beato Angelico' and unite him closely with the customary conception of Florentine painting: a mélange of Gothic elegance and inner meaning, and the solid form and management of colour in the Renaissance.

European character, like the mature Romanesque in the twelfth and early thirteenth centuries, or the final court phase of Gothic, early in the fifteenth century. At the outset this artistic and cultural movement could still be regarded as being on a local scale, favoured by a happy constellation of political rulers (the Medici Dynasty), general economic prosperity (Early and Financial Capitalism, plus an organized banking system) and a rich reservoir of creative skills. Within little less than a generation and in astonishingly close succession, the city produced over a dozen artistically gifted individuals, who could all in hindsight claim world stature. To mention only the most outstanding, Brunelleschi was born in 1377; Lorenzo Ghiberti a year later in 1378; Donatello a decade later in 1386; and a year after that Fra Angelico.

Shortly before came the great painter Masolino, in 1383. In another decade there followed Michelozzo (1396) and Paolo Uccello (1397). At brief intervals these were joined by Masaccio (1401), Leon Battista Alberti (1404) and Filippo Lippi (1406). Benozzo Gozzoli in 1420 and Castagno in 1423 brought this important biographical sequence to a close.

Like Dante's *dolce stil nuovo* just one hundred and fifty years previously, the new style soon spread beyond Florence to the whole of Italy and the entire European world. From Brunelleschi onward the world learned to think differently about architecture. Donatello and Ghiberti developed canonical rules for sculpture which apply even up to the present. After Masolino, Masaccio, Lippi and Castagno, painters were forced to look at the world with new eyes, and before Vasari even, the great theorist Alberti laid down rules for a doctrine of art and aesthetics which are still binding to-day. The forces then operating in Florence, with a concentration that was extraordinary, produced one invention after another, the artistic side being only one aspect among others. In the field of economic theory, political science, linguistics and poetics, the exact sciences and medicine, the Arno city was no less productive and was already being compared by contemporaries to Ancient Greece and styled 'The New Athens'. Referring to the painter Pisanello from Verona (1397–1450), who was reconciling Gothic and Renaissance, a contemporary witness has succinctly outlined, in less than a dozen concepts, the artistic programme of these enormously productive decades. Angiolo Galli, writing in 1442 of Pisanello, defined the new 'cult of the beautiful' during the Renaissance as: *'Arte, mesura, aere et desegno, manera, prospectiva et naturale gli ha dato el celo per mirabil dono.'* Literally translated this phrase is flat and almost devoid of meaning: 'The Heavens bestowed on him [Pisanello] a miraculous gift: art, restraint, air and draughtsmanship, manner, perspective and nature.' More fully expressed each one of these concepts has a precise procedural meaning.

Arte signifies artistic skill, perfection in a new, independent sense extending beyond the medieval crafts. *Mesura,* measure or restraint, refers to the wide area encompassing the new doctrine of proportion and composition, the aesthetics of order, based on new mathematical and scientific knowledge, i.e. harmony that can be measured, determining equally the construction of a painted or sculpted human nude; an architectural structure; a piece of music; a poem successful metrically; or the rotation of the stars in their spheres. Here we have art made science, and conversely science made into art, an ideal which was to govern the Renaissance up to the sixteenth century, and art from then on until our own day. *Aere,* air, is to be taken as aerial perspective, i.e. sensitivity to atmospheric phenomena in painting, the grading of colour by perspective in open landscapes, while *desegno,* or *disegno,* the doctrine of the 'correct' anatomical or perspective drawing of a human nude or a figural composition or of architecture and scenery, was of course the Florentine contribution to Italian Renaissance art. This has been mentioned before in connection with the 'graphism' of the Florentine incrustation style. Later on, in the sixteenth century, Italian art theory, as in Vasari, will connect up the doctrine of *disegno* with the concept of the ideal artist, at the same time characterizing the two great centres of Italian art around 1550, 'graphic' Florence and 'painting' Venice, as complementary artistic possibilities. The ideal artist was required to have *il colore di Titiano e il disegno di Michelangelo*—'the colour of [the Venetian] Titian, and the drawing of [the Florentine] Michelangelo'. *Manera,* style, means lightness of touch, the actual technical means, obediently and effortlessly to hand as a matter of course. No one wishing to play late Beethoven sonatas should have to worry about fingering. Any humanist or philologist interpreting Plato must know his vocabulary. No one who, like Pisanello, wants to master large-scale, exceedingly detailed scenes containing many figures can afford to have any problems as regards the technique of pigments, supplies of paint, or choice of the right brush, and the smooth execution of commissions for portraits. Fifty to seventy years later the High Renaissance and Mannerism summed all this up under the concept of the *virtuoso*, a tireless creator who is absolutely sure of his means. Since then virtuosity has become a proof, though not the only one, of artistic quality. *Prospectiva* probably means the newly-discovered linear perspective, based on precise geometric construction. In Early Renaissance paintings in Florence the linear base-points can often be recognized scratched into the background as a construction aid. Dürer has gone into this in detail, basing himself on the preparatory work of Italian theorists like Francesco di Giorgio Martini and Paolo Uccello. The *prospectiva* leads to a new organization of picture space, which now becomes the real space of living experience. No succession of flat, stratified side-scenes remains as in the painting of the entire Middle Ages. *Naturale*, finally, must be translated as meaning truth to nature, nearness to nature, the study of nature, and not as 'naturalism', which was already familiar to Gothic artists.

To sum up, these acquired skills and inherited talents are termed 'gifts from Heaven'. The artist was thereby raised to the status of an exceptional and special phenomenon. His new social rank was decided, beyond the crafts, outside the guilds and beyond normal reproduction of human life. Anyone possessed of Heavenly gifts, so obviously distinguished, stands on a par with the educated and propertied classes, with the patrician who has money and knows Greek, or with the ruler who has political power and soldiers at his command. It is not far from this to the highest distinction which the art critics of the High Renaissance could bestow, namely *'divino'*, or 'divine' artist. Michelangelo was so judged, and Raphael and Titian, that constellation of three divine shining lights. This conception of the artist reaches its peak in the story according to which Emperor Charles V, ruler of a kingdom 'on which the sun never set', was sitting for a portrait by Titian and is said to have picked up the painter's brush when in his concentration the latter let it slip. As he did so he bowed, in the gesture of a servant: the Sovereign on Earth kneeling before the Sovereign in the Kingdom of Art.

This relationship of equality, almost of equality of rank, between artists and their eminent patrons was no one-sided affair. It was not only the social position and evaluation of the artist that altered with the Renaissance, or artistic activity that freed itself as something autonomous and special from the 'humiliations' of the medieval crafts. The converse was also true. Learned or rich patrons among the humanist-trained commercial patricians and bearers of political authority also approached the artistic style of existence, became artists themselves, or at least understood a great deal about art. 'Dilettante' was a complimentary term at the time.

Here too it was Florence in the fifteenth century that began it all. The new evaluation of the artist's work and of the artist himself, as having an important role to play in social life, came in the Early Renaissance period from Florence. 'Here, for the first time, the leaders of State recognise the spiritual equality of artists, because they are artists themselves.' (H. Keller, 1960.) We know that Lorenzo 'il Magnifico' Medici made with his own hands an architectural model for the castle of Poggio Reale near Naples. Giovanni de' Medici took part, with his own model, in the final competition in 1587 for the façade of Florence's cathedral. Relations between the Medici and 'their' artists were generally friendly and always on the basis of colleague to colleague.

Michelozzo, the architect and sculptor, accompanied Cosimo de' Medici into temporary exile in Venice in 1434. His sons were brought up in the Medici palace in the city and attained high office as bishop and lawyer. The architectural 'dynasty' of the Sangallos and the Medicis maintained a godfather relationship. Cosimo 'the Elder' Medici and Donatello were demonstrably close friends. The fifteen-year-old, highly-gifted Michelangelo was taken into Lorenzo Medici's household as a *familiaris*, had his own room in the palace and shared the family table. Bertoldo, the sculptor in bronze, also had a touching relationship with Lorenzo Medici. He had his own studio in the palace, in which he slept; often accompanied his princely friend to the mineral baths; was treated by Lorenzo's private doctor, the best

Pages 56 and 57:
31 Fra Angelico: 'The Deposition from the Cross' (cut slightly at the edges). Florence. San Marco Museum. This altarpiece, which was painted from about 1435 to 1440, is a good example of Fra Angelico's style. The Gothic spirit still underlies the elegantly stylized figures, but the draughtsmanship, which is finely conceived in three dimensions, and the sturdy arrangement of the many figures in the composition expresses the Renaissance creative impulse. The landscape in the background—a glimpse of a fortified hill town on the left-hand side and on the right a densely populated valley with a castle on a hilltop—is a typical blend of idealized features and precise observation. The medieval gold background has disappeared and we look out on to the open fifteenth-century landscape as if through a window, with white clouds drifting in the summer sky, trees drawn with botanical accuracy and proper spacing to give perspective. The bright, transparent, resonant colouring, with clearly delineated areas of natural colour and blue and red dominant colours as it were in contrapposto, *is characteristic of Florentine painting.*

REX·IVDEORV.
GLORI

in the country; and in one of the Medici's country villas, where he had been taken when mortally ill on account of the good air, died mourned by the princely clan like a close member of the family. Intimate relations such as these between artist and patron were common later throughout sixteenth-century Italy. The close contact in Florence between the power-élite and leading artists is an expression of the public character which art was able to claim in the Late Middle Ages, and of the great public interest aroused among all classes. One sign of this was the Florentine-Tuscan habit of holding competitions for all important public commissions, a novelty in Italian art-history but typical of the cultural scene in Tuscany. The first great competitions for building the Cathedral, at the end of the thirteenth and beginning of the fourteenth centuries, have already been described. This continued in the fifteenth and sixteenth centuries. The lists of commission members in 1490, 1498 and 1504 for the various competitions have been preserved and are interesting and illuminating as to the class-free nature of public opinion. The 1504 competition had been announced on the occasion of setting up Michelangelo's 'David' (Plate 56) in the choir-section of the Cathedral. Later it was the existing site in front of the Palazzo Vecchio that was selected (Plate 16). The lists contain a cross-section of the city's social structure and truly reflect public participation in matters of art. In addition to the most famous of the city's artists, the architects of the Sangallo family and (in the 1504 jury) Leonardo da Vinci, they included, literally, 'butcher, baker and candlestick-maker': several joiners, a few goldsmiths, a mason, a stonemason, a smith, the town-crier and town-piper, plus a few jewellers, a painter of miniatures and a carpet manufacturer.

The artificially charged atmosphere of the city, with the economic climate favouring art and providing splendid opportunities for commissions, not only for 'high' art but for applied art and handicrafts in particular, attracted hordes of major and minor artists from 1450 onwards. The surviving lists of guilds from about 1470 show in the case of Florence seventy butchers and slaughterers, sixty-six grocers and eighty-three silk workers. Parallel with these we find eighty-four craft workshops devoted to wood-carving and inlaid work, fifty-four studios for marble and stone décor and forty-four gold- and silversmiths, an astonishingly equal distribution as regards status. The position is no different among the 'authentically' great artists, except that their story is rather confused, since many of the names of artists that have come down to us cannot be linked to works that have been preserved, and the historical process of selection and destruction has meant that they and their *Oeuvre* have been consigned to oblivion. The St. Luke Guild of *artistes-peintres* numbered in 1472 thirty professional 'figure-painters'. Of these only eight can be historically traced. No fewer than seventeen bearing the name 'Raffaelo' are testified to in Florence from the beginning of the sixteenth century, one of these being the 'divine' Raphael Santi.

Since the artists pouring into the city could no longer organize themselves inside the narrow specialized framework of the appointed guilds of medieval origin, and did not feel themselves to be artisans any more, they chose the guild to which they wanted to belong, freely, on the basis of social prestige and the social achievements of the various 'unions'. This contrasts with the limited freedom of choice offered in the unions of to-day. In 1517 nine plastic artists were accepted into the guild of the *medici e speziali,* Physicians and Apothecaries, probably because the *speziali* were also druggists, and dealt in pigments and other artists' requirements. One of the finest of addresses—best compared with that of an exclusive London club—was that of the Arte della Lana, the Wool-Weavers Guild. Not surprisingly, the names of prominent artists are to be found on their rolls. No little influence was required, as well as recognition of one's work, to achieve entry into this distinguished assembly, which had desirable commissions to distribute or procure. It is no accident that the Arte della Lana was the only guild to describe its headquarters in 1427 as a *palazzo* (palace), equal, therefore, to the Palazzo del Vescovo (the Bishop's residence), the Palazzo della Signoria (City Hall) or the Bargello

32 Filippino Lippi 'Resurrection, after fourteen years, of the dead Son of Emperor Theophilus by St. Peter', painted from 1483–1485. Florence. Santa Maria del Carmine: Brancacci Chapel. The painting belongs to the series of frescoes depicting the life of St. Peter which was begun by Masaccio and Masolino and completed by Lippi from approximately 1483 to 1485. Masaccio took part in the work depicted, the figural composition, at least, being traceable to him, though the heads are said to be by Lippi. The Imperial Prince's head is represented by that of a young Florentine noble (Granacci). Masaccio's frescoes in the Brancacci Chapel introduce the new 'classical' Renaissance style based on Greco-Roman models, while the art of Fra Angelico and his colleagues represents a counter-current within Florentine painting in 1440–1450 which is historically minded and Gothic. In this sense the earlier work of Masaccio and his circle can be said to be more 'modern', and it can easily be understood that the young artists of the High Renaissance in Florence, Michelangelo and Leonardo da Vinci in particular, should have had their schooling in the creations of Masaccio and Masolino.

33

(city government), whereas all the other 'union' simply had a *casa* (house). Nor was it an accident that the same guild was given responsibility in 1331 for the most outstanding (and problematic) public construction project in the city, the building of the Cathedral, for people were well aware that only the Rectors of the powerful Wool-Weavers Guild, with its financial and organizing skill and its political authority in the commune, could still rescue the whole enterprise, which was constantly being brought to a standstill. Two hundred years later the Guild did in fact bring the cathedral to completion without further complications. Similar sponsorships were undertaken by other guilds in Florence for other centenary projects, including the Foundlings' Hospital, the San Marco Monastery and so on. That this was by no means a purely Italian phenomenon can be seen from the fact that Strasbourg Cathedral was also completed under guild supervision and the Rathaus and towers in Cologne were similarly completed. All the important guilds in Florence got together in the end to make it possible for Orsanmichele to be garnished with statuary. (Plate 52). No description of the rediscovery of the Graeco-Roman freestanding figure by Donatello, Ghiberti, Michelozzo and Nanni di Banco in the early decades of the fifteenth century, which entered into fertile competition with the draped Gothic style, would be complete without mention in Florentine records of the guilds of stonemasons and joiners, stocking-weavers and butchers, linen-weavers, harness-makers,

33 Filippino Lippi: 'The SS. Peter and Paul before the Proconsul' (detail), circa 1483–85. Florence, Carmine Church, Brancacci Chapel. This frescoe is to be placed in the same context as the previous illustration. Here too, Lippi followed in the footsteps of Masaccio and Massolino. The head of Simon Magus (far left) is probably a portrait of the painter Antonio del Pollaiuole, whereas the young man (above right) could be a self-portrait of Filippino Lippi himself.

34 Filippino Lippi: 'Apparition of the virgin to St. Bernard', circa *1480, Florence, Badia Church. This altarpainting of the vision of St. Bernard is one of Lippi's most outstanding early paintings. The figures have a nearly sculptural plasticity and sharpness of contours. The brilliant portrait of the donor, Domenico del Pugliese (below right), the depiction of the various members of his family and the group of the Madonna with angels are tell-tale examples of the Florentine art of representation. The rugged rock-landscape provides further evidence of the sense of reality, inherent to Florentine painting on the threshold of the High-Rennaissance.*

34

furriers and wool-weavers who here immortalized their patrons and thereby provided the artists who revived the art of sculpture with an appropriate basis for their innovatory performance.

The public character of art and, conversely, the public's feeling for art in fifteenth and sixteenth century Florence, which was both the cause and effect of the incomparable cultural climate there during the Renaissance, is illustrated by contemporary anecdotes, which throw a more significant light

ΕΛΕΗΣ
ΚΑΤΑΤ

on the scene between 1450 and 1550 than any prolonged analysis. In 1501 Leonardo, as was the custom, publicly exhibited in his studio the cartoon for his celebrated 'St. Anne with Two Others'. Public reaction to this event has been described by Giorgio Vasari, whom we have already had occasion to mention several times: 'It was not only artists who were moved to admire the work. When the cartoon was ready men and women, young and old, could be seen for two whole days making their pilgrimage to the room in order to contemplate Leonardo's marvellous achievement, as if it were all some brilliant festival. The entire population was astonished. 'The same scene was repeated fifty years later with Benvenuto Cellini's famous bronze statue of "Perseus", a masterpiece of mature mannerism, which was completed in 1553–1554 and now graces the Loggia dei Lanzi, by the Palazzo Vecchio and the Uffizi (Plate 66). Shortly before its completion Duke Cosimo Medici suggested to the artist that the work should be exhibited in the studio for a few hours and made the subject of discussion, in order to test public opinion. Cellini did not like the idea but complied with his patron's wish and—lo and behold!—Cellini's fears proved groundless. 'On the day when the Perseus was placed on public exhibition over twenty sonnets were at once affixed to the door. Even when the statue was no longer on show the shower of Greek and Latin verses continued unabated, for the University of Pisa was on holiday at the time, and Florentine students who were staying at home found this demonstration of poetic training a most agreeable way of spending their time. Well-known artists like Pontormo and Bronzino also affixed their adulations in verse to the studio-door.' (H. Keller, 1960.)

After this excursion into Florentine art-sociology let us return to the 'Great Period', between 1420 and 1450.

It is scarcely possible to render a systematic account of these years or of their inventiveness. The best way to master the series of artistic innovations would be to list them in tabular form, like a catalogue, for most of what for us constitutes the artistic, architectural and sculptural inheritance was then new and unusual and had perforce to be regarded as 'invention'.

When Goethe shared the experience of the Feast of the Epiphany in Rome at the beginning of 1787, in the Propaganda Fide with its confusion of tongues, and heard the first sounds in the language of Plato and Euripides, he acknowledged that 'The sound of Greek was like the shining of a star at night.' The Florentines must have felt the same in 1400 when the first of the émigrés arrived from Byzantium and talked to each other in their native tongue. Goethe's enthusiasm is on a par with the delight in life felt by the first Florentine artists to glance into the well of the classical past and discover there their personal and artistic identity—or rediscover it, we have to say, in the Renaissance sense. Vasari clearly reports how Brunelleschi and his friend Donatello the sculptor set out for Rome between 1420 and 1430, armed with stadia rods, measuring-lines and spades; how they very patiently studied the ruins that were still standing; took measurements and made surveys; discussed their purpose and proportions; and probably dug up foundations, half-buried capitals and drum-like columns, which must have scared away the cows and sheep that grazed among the fields of ruins in the heart of Rome and on the Forum, significantly known in the local dialect as the *campo vacchino*. The two friends' mysterious activity and peculiar equipment appeared highly suspicious to the Romans, who took them for conspirators, or—closer to home—treasure-hunters.

The study of nature—and here we recall Angiolo Galli's concept *naturale*—and of the ancient world are the two poles between which art in Florence henceforth moved. It was out of the ancient world and nature that the new style grew and was at once accepted as the national Italian style and as the source of a new national, political identity. Vasari's tirades a century later against the 'barbaric' Gothic of the North now become comprehensible. It was not simply the result of a 'generation gap' between two fundamentally different art eras and styles but also the expression of native identity, which had to be delimited and defended like any other national identity. The

Page 62:
35 Domenico Ghirlandaio: 'St. Jerome in his Sanctum', 1480. Florence. Ognissanti Church. This fresco, dated 1480, shows St. Jerome in his study of the period. He is presented as a Florentine humanist at work in his studiolo, *with all the attributes of spiritual activity.*

Page 63:
36 Sandro Botticelli: St. Augustine, circa *1480. Florence. Ognissanti Church. This mural of 1480 belongs in the same context as the previous illustration and is the companion picture of Ghirlandaio's 'St. Jerome'. St. Augustine is also seated in a contemporary humanist study. He is gazing in reverie at a celestial globe. It does not seem an accident that those who commissioned the painting were the Florentine Vespuccis. Amerigo Vespucci came from this family, and explored the 'New World' following the trail left by Columbus. It now bears his name: America.*

37

37 Andrea del Sarto: 'St. Filippo Benizzi healing a Woman possessed.' (Detail). 1510. Florence. Santissima Annunziata. Passage in the Outer Court. The painting derives from a series of frescoes dated 1510 and represents the Florentine contribution to High Renaissance painting. Del Sarto's cycle is distinguished particularly by attractive landscape backgrounds, which can be glimpsed through the architectural framework (just visible at the upper edges).

individuality, complexity and originality which the generation of Brunelleschi and Donatello found in the works of the ancients and in the living works of nature now became qualities in artistic creation and characteristics of the artistic individual himself, i.e. of the complex *uomo universale* of the Renaissance.

The 'new style' encompassed equally and uniformly the three most important artistic categories, architecture, painting and sculpture. Contemporaries must already have been aware of this. A favourite game among the Florentine intellectuals, an area, as it were, in which art criticism could be assessed with the weapons of the shrewdest methodology and scientific fantasy, was the *paragone,* comparison of the arts with one another. This involved a question which was passionately debated. To which of the three categories could leading role be given? The plastic arts could, for instance, reproduce the human figure, the central theme of the Renaissance, in palpable three-dimensional form, and the resemblance would be totally convincing. An ancient story would be trotted out as proof according to which a cow painted by Apelles, or cast in bronze by Myron, had been so lifelike that a steer had wanted to mount it. To the 'new' philosophy of fidelity to nature this was an indication of artistic quality. The sculptor, on the other hand, was unable to represent the human ambience and atmospheric phenomena, except in the background of bas-reliefs almost painterly in treatment, and even there only very inadequately. Painting again can convey

38

any mood in flowing colour washes and atmospheric tones. It can give the illusion of perspective and depth, but is obliged to represent physical volume and plasticity in terms of light and shade, and sometimes the only view of the human body it gives is one that is posed, stiff and as if fixed in whatever stance suits the 'tableau'. It is to the *paragone* idea (typical of the all-embracing principle of rivalry and competition that was the essence of Florentine art) that we are indebted for such profound thinking concerning the nature of art and the arts in general. This friendly argument was never settled. Even Vasari was unable to give a satisfactory answer to a question that was basically insoluble. Each of the three categories posed new problems conditioned by social, religious and political changes. A new language of form was found for these, and new techniques and materials discovered or developed from methods and materials handed down from the Middle Ages.

A leading place was allotted from about 1420 to the great Filippo Brunelleschi and that at a time when in the rest of Europe the Soft Style,

38 Lorenzo Ghiberti: 'The Sacrifice of Isaac', 1402. Florence. Bargello, National Museum. This bronze relief is one of the gems of the Florentine National Museum. Along with Brunelleschi's 'Sacrifice of Isaac' (illustration following), it was awarded the prize as the best entry in the 1401–1402 competition for the doors of the Florentine San Giovanni Baptistery, but not transferred there, as constituting a 'model example'. This work is the beginning of the breakthrough to the 'new style' in Florence, in reaction to Gothic tradition. Notice the treatment of the upper part of Isaac's body, anatomically accurate and owing everything to classical art; also the dramatic composition, in tense counterpoint.

39

39 Filippo Brunelleschi: 'The Sacrifice of Isaac', 1402. Florence, Bargello, National Museum. This sculpture is one of the two 'competition reliefs' for the Florence Baptistery (see previous illustration) that have been preserved. Like Ghiberti's 'Sacrifice of Isaac' it shows mastery of the bronze-casting technique developed from ancient sources, and perfect handling of the central problem of the art of relief, the tension between 'figure' and 'background'.

Court Gothic, still prevailed. As an architect in particular, but also as a sculptor, he produced a new vocabulary of form, starting out from the theoretical and empirical preoccupation with the ancient world (archaeological expeditions to Rome). At that time many more monuments were still standing than there are to-day. Brunelleschi convinced himself and his colleagues that what they had before them was a treasure of inestimable value which had always been available but had escaped attention for centuries owing to the fog produced by 'barbaric' Gothic. 'Brunelleschi was the first clearly to recognise pure gold, so to speak, in this treasure and decided to make out of it a coinage which would drive out of circulation the worn currency of architectural language which had thus far been valid; this seemed to him to have become devalued because of base medieval elements.' (W. Paatz, 1953).

One main result of the Roman studies by Brunelleschi and Donatello was the re-introduction of the four classical orders: 'Doric' (or 'Tuscan');

40

40, 41 Lorenzo Ghiberti: first bronze door on the north side of the Baptistery of San Giovanni in Florence. The door resulted from a competition held in 1401–02 in which Ghiberti's design was chosen in preference to Brunelleschi's. It was executed during the years 1403–1424, with the help of assistants. It follows Graeco-Roman models in the way the three-dimensional decoration has 'crept' from the doorcasing on to the actual door panels. In the temples of classical antiquity, too, artists liked to decorate the portals with figurative decoration.

'Ionian'; 'Corinthian'; and 'Composite'. These were indisputably to govern the whole of architecture from 1420 up to the advent of functionalism and the Bauhaus in our own time. The Greek and Roman system of load and support, columns, free-standing pillars, wall-panelling and beams or rounded arches now replaced the aspiring Gothic, which was increasingly criticised by the Renaissance theorists as 'contrary to nature'. A series of ideal forms based on Euclidean geometry, such as the cube, sphere, cylinder or hemisphere, was used instead, as the main architectural framework. The central cupola became the monumental *leit-motiv,* built up on the ideal shape of the circle as in Florence's Cathedral, where Brunelleschi's imposing volume was first brought to such a pitch of mastery that the Dome—'the Roof of Florence'—now lies lightly over the city, at once centralizing and protecting (Plates 1 and 5). The return to ideal shapes, 'original forms' we might say, had a metaphysical basis for early Renaissance artists. Architecture was regarded as 'petrified music', a contrived metaphor for the harmony of the spheres. This 'harmonic aesthetic of order', as the art historians who followed this school of thought paraphrased it, implied a major revolution, particularly in ecclesiastical architecture, which continued to be seen as the highest form of

41

architecture. The Florentine Cathedral Dome (Plate 5), and finally—one of the most perfect, solid and harmonious creations in Florentine architecture—the Pazzi Chapel by Santa Croce (Plate 11), represent the new style. These are all creations of the protean Brunelleschi whose structures did not merely introduce a new chapter in art history but decisively altered Florence's image and left his personal stamp upon it. Following the new Renaissance claims to universality, Brunelleschi invariably thought in terms of wider urban contexts. Thus the harmonious cupolas of Brunelleschi and his successors fit into the Florence profile as a contrast to the sheer towers and façade motifs of the Gothic: the Vecchio Tower, the Bargello and Badia Towers, and the forms assumed by the Cathedral façade, as well as Giotto's free-standing Campanile. Together with these they comprise an unmistakeable unity, pregnant with meaning. (Plate 1).

It was the human figure that provided the key to this architectural composition and proportioning. Leonardo's figure of a man, proportioned-out and with arms and legs outstretched, encircled as in a gyro wheel, is now well-known. The axes of the body divide the circle into four sections. Theorists described the human form, as a proportioned basic figure, in terms of columns. The head then becomes the capital, the trunk the shaft of columns, the greatest projection being in the centre, around the navel; while the feet are the columns' base. Alternatively the human nude was outlined in the basic design of a basilica (Head = apse; breast = crossing; outstretched arms = transepts; legs = nave). These analogies between human and architectural proportions established a direct relationship between the 'microcosm' and the 'macrocosm' and between the earthly and celestial spheres, a typical Renaissance conception. Architecture, the symbol of both heavenly harmony and organic human proportions, thus became the medium for expressing a comprehensive cosmic idea.

This theory of organic and ideal proportions coinciding answered the two decisive ideals of Renaissance aesthetics, firstly the classical, which had made man 'the measure of all things', and secondly the return to the world of nature and the organic, to naturalness (Galli's *naturale*).

In a never-ending attempt to get to grips with classical antiquity and with nature, artists tried to trace the secret laws of proportion by empirical observation and ingenious speculation; to fathom the undoubted beauty of classical ruins, which people were not prepared simply to feel, but wanted also to decipher and imitate scientifically. The ancient basic principles of *contrapposto* and Golden Section were recovered. The principle of the unity of opposites *(contrapposto)* or of harmony between the height and breadth of a wall surface, pictorial area or figural composition (medial Section) were decisive factors in architecture, painting and sculpture.

The ancient ruins, however, not only stimulated the scientific ambitions of the archaeologists and exalted national sentiments in the contemplation of the former greatness of Rome and Italy, but also fostered nostalgic and elegiac feelings, a sense of the former, now irrecoverable spirit of the past and of a 'Golden Age' bound up with Roman times and idealized; an age which in fancy became a long-buried Utopia. Yet there was always an awareness that this kingdom of beauty, dignity, virtue and identity with the *'patria'* could never be recaptured, however much Florence was ennobled, or the Pope in Rome was styled the new 'Imperator Romanorum' in an ecclesiastical empire of Faith and Spirit. Petrarch and Boccaccio both voice feelings such as these. From the fifteenth century onward accounts mount up of learned men of letters visiting Rome's ruins and being transported into a trance-like state by the ancient city; musing on the Colosseum in the sparkling midday heat, or on the Temple of Venus in the luminous evening glow; conversing with the most illustrious spirits of antiquity—Cicero the orator, Cato the moralist, the great Caesar, the Emperor Augustus, or the stoic philosopher Seneca—among the rows of tombs in the Via Appia, shaded by laurel, cypress and plane-tree.

In this atmosphere it caused a world-wide sensation when on April 18 1485, some fifty years after Donatello's and Brunelleschi's alleged stay in Rome, the news ran like wildfire through the city (and soon through the other Italian centres) that Lombard masons looking for treasure on the Via Appia, not far from the celebrated monument to Caecilia Metella, had broken into an ancient tomb. They had at once come upon a marble sarcophagus bearing the inscription: 'Julia, daughter of Claudius'. Taking with them the valuable grave gifts—gold and jewellery—the grave-robbers disappeared, leaving behind quite a different kind of treasure for the rapturous Romans who soon

42 Donatello (?): 'John the Baptist'. Florence. Bargello, National Museum. The attribution to Donatello of this figure, which combines an attitude that is still Gothic (the motif of the hand) with a fully Renaissance anatomy—scientific and precisely observed (see the collarbone and feet)—is now being disputed all over again. Some experts have even suggested that it is the work of the young Michelangelo, in which case the marble sculpture could be dated to the 1490s at the earliest.

43 Donatello: 'David'. 1430–1432. Florence. Bargello, National Museum. This sculpture, carved in 1430–1432, was originally intended for a fountain in the Palazzo Vecchio. Donatello's masterpiece is generally considered to be the most important piece of sculpture dating from this period. *(For a complete description see page 79.)*

42

43

44 Donatello: Annunciation Relief, 1435. Florence. Santa Croce. This central work by Donatello, standing only a few yards from Michelangelo's tomb, was created as an altar-tabernacle in 1435 under commission from the Cavalcanti family. The two-figured group is wonderfully tender in spiritual expression, revealing the tense relations between the Madonna and the Angel. The architecture of the framework is based on classical models (the aedicula motif), as are the two pink terra cotta putti next to the scrolled pediment at the upper edge of the picture. The two figures (rediscovered only in 1900) imitate classical figurative acroteria, which were also usually of pinkish clay. The original gold paint on the greenish stone was carefully touched up in 1884.

45 Donatello: Bronze pulpit. Florence. San Lorenzo. The two bronze pulpits, only one of which is illustrated here, are in the style of late Classical/Early Christian 'ambos' and thus link up with classical tradition. Donatello did not live to see the completion of the two structures, which were finished by Bertoldo and Bellano between 1460 and 1470. The marble column supports are a mannerist addition. Originally the twin pulpits probably stood on a wooden framework.

45

discovered the sacrilege. According to contemporary reports the sarcophagus contained the well-preserved corpse of a young woman, almost a child, some fifteen years old, her expression so alive still as to make it seem that she had only just passed away. The limbs were still quite flexible and owing to the finest of embalming materials and fixatives the living colour of the skin, the half-open eyes and the mouth, opened as if to speak, were in a complete state of preservation. The body was solemnly escorted to the palace of the Curator in the Capitol and placed on public exhibition. Then a veritable pilgrimage began of men, women and youths, as if to some masterpiece by Leonardo or Michelangelo, and the stream of sightseers never let up. Even artists came, to take her likeness, for—how could it be otherwise?—the dead girl, reborn so to speak, was as charming in her loveliness as Venus the Goddess of Love herself. In the words of a late fifteenth-century eye-witness she was 'beautiful beyond the power of words or description, and if words or description were possible, no one who had not seen her would believe them.' Pope Innocent VIII felt after a few days that the spectacle had gone on long enough, and put an end to the beauty-cult which for him—despite all his own enthusiasm for classical antiquity—was threatening to assume features that were clearly pagan. He therefore had the body secretly buried without ceremony at an obscure spot in front of the Porta Pinciano. The empty sarcophagus remained in the Palazzo dei Conservatori, and was for a long time still sought out in awe by disciples of beauty fascinated by the ancient world. The memory of that event in 1485 remained so alive that when after the war the comparatively well-preserved body of a woman of the ancient world came to light on the Via Cassia, people believed and insisted on believing that what they had before them was the girl from the Via Appia whom Innocent VIII had put away. *Se non è vero, è ben trovato,* as they say in Italy. Even if it isn't true, it's still a good story, and illustrates the popular mentality at the start of the Renaissance, which hungered after just such myths and legends. It is a matter of indifference whether it really was an aristocratic woman of Ancient Rome who was found, as the Renaissance believed, or whether—as Jacob Burckhardt claims—her fresh appearance was due to a wax mask; or even whether some Egyptian merchant in love had had a little Syrian dancer

artistically embalmed by the methods used in his own country.

The treasures discovered in libraries and archives when looking through ancient writings were of a quite different kind. The yellowed and neglected parchments were just as eagerly hunted down and removed from their dusty tombs as the 'Via Appia beauty', and studied as authentic evidence of the Golden Age of the arts. Every hint in these manuscripts, which were without illustrations, was followed up, and attempts were made to picture the classical forms of decoration and architecture in order to test them out on new buildings. This became particularly evident when a type of building peculiar to the Middle Ages had to be remodelled to conform to the new age: the metropolitan Palazzo, which was the most important assignment in secular architecture, ranking now alongside the ecclesiastical. Transforming the enclosed cube-shaped palace structure by means of cloister-like inner courtyards surrounded by open loggias, which fourteenth century had developed in the Palazzo Vecchio (Plates 16 and 17) or the Bargello (Plate 19), Michelozzo created in Florence in 1444 the prototype in Italy of the Renaissance palace, whose imprint can still be felt in the Roman High Baroque period.

This was the Palazzo Medici (Plates 20 and 21). True, the block-type construction was retained for traditional and representational as well as security reasons (the inner part of the city was still by no means pacified), but it expressed the power and dignity of the politically important families in a way that everyone could understand. The façade, however, was transformed in line with the new principles derived from ruins and the Graeco-Roman theory of art. The mass of the façade henceforth produced the basic architectural problem: statics, support, load, structure of floors from base, main zone and terminal zone. The ground floor, bearer of the greatest load and the link with the ground, displayed its function in a rugged band of large rusticated ashlar left in its rough state at the front. This term comes from the Latin *rusticus*, rustic, country-style, sturdy, smooth. Sturdy, earthy and resistant, like a memory of the defensive constructions of the medieval town-palaces, the pedestal area props up the first floor with finely-formed smoothed

46 Donatello: 'Cantoria', 1433–1439. Florence. Cathedral Museum. Donatello's marble Singing Gallery for the Cathedral in Florence (1433–1439) comes to life in a Bacchic series of putti representing angels dancing and exulting in honour of the Blessed Virgin, Patroness of the Cathedral and protector of the City; and in the ornamental motif, quite in the spirit of the Classical Renaissance.

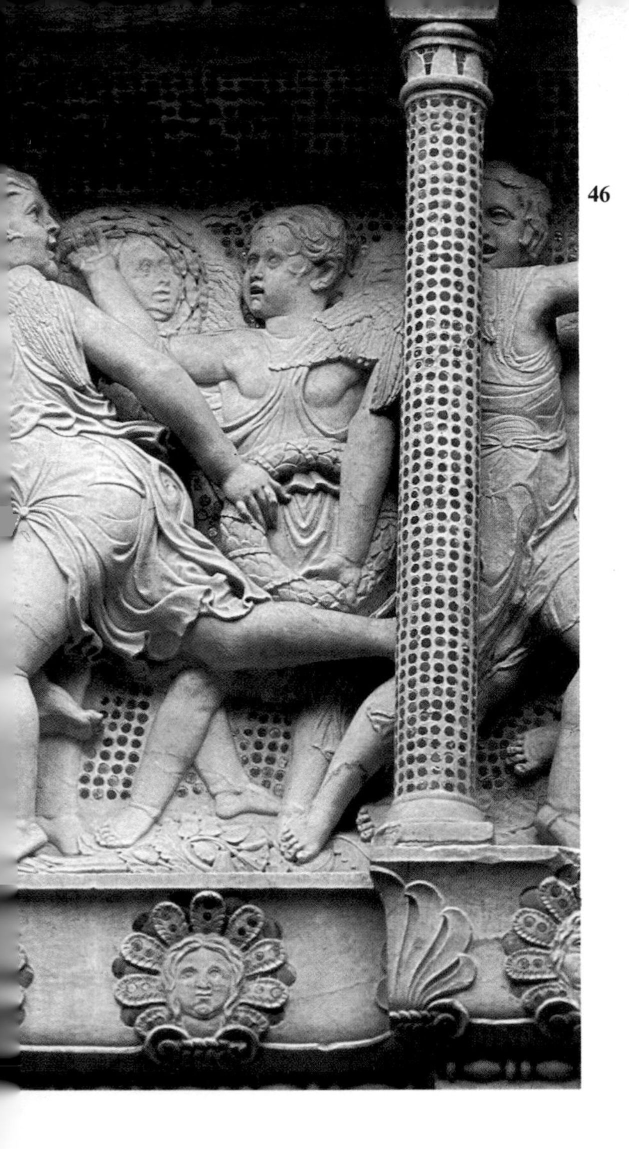

46

squared stone, the grooving of which is still clear and separate. On the highest floor the wall becomes a tense membrane, the band of squared stone being apparent only after a second glance at the hair-thin seams. An imposing heavy layer of festooned cornice, counteracting the lightness of the upper storey in *contrapposto*, rounds everything off and traps in deep shadow the force striving upwards. The cornice is built up in the classical manner from classic consoles. The windows stand in regular symmetrical axes and a Renaissance *leit-motiv* appears on the ground floor, caught up by semi-circular blind arches: the aedicula window, with a classical, triangular pediment above classical-looking brackets. With certain deviations—the Palazzo Strozzi, for instance, the latest in our series, begun in 1485 by Benedetto da Maiano (Plate 24), has a classical dentil frieze as floor-division—this type remained the rule for centuries in Florence and throughout Italy, as in the Pitti Palace, which was begun by Luca Fancelli in 1457 from plans by Brunelleschi and not completed until 1650 (Plates 22 and 23).

The inner courts of the Medici and Strozzi Palaces display a calculated, refined contrast to the forbidding authoritarianism of the exterior (Plates 21 and 25). They are friendly and inviting, with light finely-worked arcades, entirely classical in appearance. Ornamental arrangements of columns with classical capitals have 'ideal' elegantly-profiled semi-circular arches and, as decoration, classical round medallions framing the reliefs in the Medici Palace, plus ingenious emblems. We can be sure that the Florentine builders of 1450 to 1480 thought they had recovered in these courtyards the ancient *atrium,* and in the deliberate contrast of inner and outer forms the fundamental principle of the classical Mediterranean house, the *casa degli antichi,* which is valid even to-day. The ponderous dignity and menacing majesty of the rusticated facades, solemnly overshadowed in the accidental light, might then correspond to the *gravitas* and *dignitas* of the town residence of the fine gentlemen of ancient Rome.

Needless to say the noble families residing in such palaces *more romano* tried to trace their origins more or less convincingly to Graeco-Roman roots. The Sienese family of the Piccolomini traced themselves to the ancient Roman Julians; the Barbo from Venice claimed to be descended from the Ahenobarbus; and the Giustiniani, from the Province of Venice, from the late Roman Emperor Justinian. The bourgeois family of Plato from Milan, academics and lawyers, naturally went back to the great Greek philosopher; the new Roman Massimi, to Q. Fabius Maximus; and the Paduan Cornaro—as one might have guessed—to the celebrated Cornelians of classical antiquity.

The Renaissance quest for fame, its personality cult and urge towards classical stylization of the individual found an ideal and flexible medium in painting which, like fifteenth-century architecture and sculpture, produced a whole host of discoveries in form and content, and in the secular sphere particularly expanded the medieval pictorial canon to include a multitude of new themes. 'The discovery of the world and of Man' was a decisive factor in painting also, which now proceeded to incorporate the landscape and architectural scenery, in other words man's material environment, as an autonomous representational content. Contemporary everyday life was portrayed in the 'genre' type of picture, or one dealing with manners and customs. The pictorial cosmos of Humanism opened up in historical painting, allegory and large-scale astrological programming a rich spectrum of newly-acquired cosmological, historical, literary, moral, philosophical and particularly classical mythological material. It was in the portrait, however, which now enjoyed a brilliant flowering, that the Early Renaissance gave of its best.

Like the other art forms painting gradually assumed a quite extraordinary public, political and even ideological function. A good example of this is revealed in 'Negation'. Not only were the splendours and achievements, the virtues and fame of outstanding men honoured and immortalized in

47

47, 48 and 49 Luca della Robbia: 'Cantoria' 1433–1438. Florence. Cathedral Museum. This enclosed singing gallery was begun at the same time as and in competition with Donatello's, but was completed a year earlier, in 1438. It also combines older fourteenth-century traditions with the new Early Renaissance spirit. As with Donatello's 'Cantoria', the purpose is not entirely clear. Probably no choir was ever set up here on account of the lack of space. It possibly housed an organ.

monumental frescoes, but negative propaganda was also conducted in 'scandalous portrayals and caricatures', where the politically defeated, those guilty of high treason and political criminals were condemned to eternal disgrace. The same Castagno who had erected an eternal monument to the mercenary Captain-General Niccolò da Tolentino in a monumental fresco happily accepted a macabre commission by the victorious Medici to exhibit the leaders of the defeated Albizzi party after the Battle of Anghiari (1440) in large tableaux on the walls of the Palace of Justice in Florence, and in the most abusive way: as dishonoured victims of execution, hanging by the feet and swaying in the air. So terrifying was its intentional effect on the townspeople that henceforth the prominent painter bore a name that was surreptitiously whispered from mouth to mouth and did him little credit: 'Andrea the Hangman'. Even the great Leonardo da Vinci undertook a similar irregular commission. He drew the Pisan Cardinal Archbishop Salviati hanged in the Palazzo Vecchio, following his execution on 26 April 1478 for taking part in the anti-Medici Pazzi conspiracy.

Violence and passion, Nature and world, womanly beauty, youthful grace and the fame of the great, esoteric allegory, classical sensuality, the fateful power of Eros—there was no theme that secular Renaissance painting could not deal with, and in each new task it created something great and never seen before.

Yet the Christian art world asserted its supremacy. The church kept on

48

49

having the most comprehensive, most attractive and best-endowed commissions to distribute, and it was in representing the Christian cosmos that Renaissance painting attained its greatest heights, transforming the basic principles of the Middle Ages in a humanist and classical sense. For this reason, and since we have space for only a limited selection, the Florence section of this volume offers only religious paintings from Florentine churches (Plates 27–37). Giotto's 'Death of St. Francis' in Santa Croce (Plate 27) has already been described in detail (Page 36). The real painting Renaissance in Florence sets in with Masaccio's famous 1425 fresco of the Trinity, in Santa Trinità (Plate 28). This innovatory achievement placed Masaccio, later unreservedly admired by the young Michelangelo and Leonardo, alongside Brunelleschi, who was twenty-four years older, and Donatello (fifteen years older).

In addition to his classically balanced composition, the masterly development of fresco technique, and the nobly sensuous characterization of the holy figures, the tragic greatness of the Blessed Virgin, the prayers of the favourite disciple John, and the majestic suffering of the crucified figure, and of God the Father supporting His Son in loving sympathy, the painting is of world stature because, in the framed and background structure of the group, a niche like a triumphal arch, Masaccio has adapted the knowledge of perspective possessed by his teacher Brunelleschi and employed it to convey a sense of majesty. Nowhere more clearly than here does the formal method of precisely constructed linear perspective appear as a 'symbolical form' (Panofsky). The guiding lines drawn by ruler in the damp finish can still be traced accurately in the picture.

Masaccio created another epoch-making work together with Masolino in the shape of the Brancacci Chapel frescoes in Santa Maria del Carmine, where an extensive series devoted to the life of St. Peter was started between

1423 and 1425 in connection with the performance of plays about the saint, which were traditional in the church. Masaccio was unable to complete the series. It was carried through from 1483 to 1485 by Filippino Lippi (Plates 32 and 33). As was his wont, in these frescoes were concealed portraits of his contemporaries: the young noble Granacci, in the person of the resurrected Imperial Prince (Plate 32); the painter Antonio Pollaiuolo; and himself, in the scene before Herod (Plate 33). So great was Masaccio's impact that the succeeding generation could not escape (nor had any desire to escape) his influence. Castagno, Botticelli and Leonardo regarded the Brancacci Chapel as their textbook in paint. Michelangelo's encounter with the genius of Masaccio left him bearing literal 'stigmata'. It was in a violent quarrel with colleagues about Masaccio that he acquired the severe facial injuries which distorted his face into a tragic mask for the rest of his life.

Quite another figure, taking us back to the fourteenth century and the world of medieval piety and spirituality, greets us in the figure of Giovanni da Fiesole, who after an eventful life found a home in the Florentine Monastery of San Marco. In the forties he created there a whole string of wall-paintings in the cells, corridors and cloisters (Plates 29 and 30). The tender spiritual expression in the faces of the angels and Madonnas, the Gothic elegance of the figures and above all the splendid, harmonious, transparent colouring with accents in light red and blue on a grand scale have made Giovanni, who entered the history of art under the name given to him by his order, Fra Angelico, one of the best-loved of painters, especially among European visitors to Florence.

At the height of this period and its ideal of humanity stand Botticelli and Ghirlandaio, with the two great companion pictures of the Church Fathers, St. Augustine and St. Jerome in Ognissanti, dating from 1480 (Plates 35 and 36). These utterly personal figures, almost portrait-like in their effect, embody the humanist *uomo universale,* the spiritual man who with passionate understanding breaks through the limits of his previous world and advances into new worlds. St. Augustine (Plate 36) is gazing thoughtfully at a celestial globe. It can be no accident that this painting was the gift of the Vespucci family from which sprang Amerigo Vespucci. Only a little later he did in actual fact open up a 'New World' which was to bear his name: America. The 'cells' of both saints are depicted as the studies of contemporaries, with a pleasure in detail that has a touch of the Netherlands, and is reminiscent of Van Eyck. We seem to be given a glimpse of a fifteenth-century studio, lacking in none of the essentials: inkwell and blotting sand, quill-pen, folios with bookmark, memoranda with notes in Greek, reading desk, spectacles, astronomical and geometrical equipment and a mathematics textbook.

The 'New Style' in Florence probably accomplished its best work in sculpture and the plastic arts. The two celebrated 'Competition Reliefs' by Ghiberti and Brunelleschi for the doors of the Florentine Baptistery (Plates 38 and 39) give a clear picture of the new classical style shortly after the turn of the century. The commission itself, the monumental bronze door with figure decoration, was a conscious link with classical antiquity. In Graeco-Roman temples, too, figurative decoration in the matter of portals had usually been restricted to the door-panels. Ghiberti's two masterpieces, the first bronze door in the 'Bel San Giovanni' from 1403 (Plates 40 and 41) and his world-famous 'Gate of Paradise', 1425, set a standard for the whole of Italy.

A significant new element was the technique of casting bronze. Bronze was quite evidently the favourite material in Renaissance sculpture and from time to time was esteemed more highly than marble in the fifteenth century. Not until Michelangelo's monumental figures, almost all of them wrested out of the 'royal' marble, was this trend reversed in the sixteenth century. Here too history was being repeated, for the writers of the ancient world have reported the importance and high technical level of bronze-casting in their day, as in the case of the Greek sculptor Myron—a legend even to the Ancient Romans—marble copies of whose renowned bronze creations such as the 'Discus Thrower' or 'Athena and Marsyas' had been traded in the Rome of antiquity.

It was certainly no coincidence, then, that probably the most epoch-making production of the period, Donatello's 'David' of 1430 in the Bargello Museum (Plate 43), was executed in this popular medium. With it the divergence of Florentine artists from the European Late Middle Ages was finally settled in favour of the new formal language. Not only is the technique new, but so is practically everything else in this enchanting figure: the formal aspect, guiding idea and spiritual expression. A well-developed, thoroughly-trained youth, still on the threshold of childhood but become a hero and a man through his deed, the vanquishing of Goliath, stands free and self-conscious, in heroic nudity before the onlooker. The rudimentary clothing, the touching straw-hat of the shepherd-boy, decorated with flowers, and the leggings, for protection against thorn-hedges, serve only to emphasize the nudity and high sensuous charm of the bare skin, on which light plays in lively reflections over the polished bronze surface. Pride, something daring and free, but an attractive embarrassment too are contained in the face of the young man, who—if we interpret the biblical story in psychological terms—is gentle and almost girlish in features, as is emphasized by the long locks. The threshold between childhood and manhood is also conveyed in the treatment of the body, which still shows soft, child-like lines, but in the sinewy arms and powerful legs illustrates the biblical figure: the mobile, light-footed shepherd who could handle the sling with unexpected strength and cunning, and who conquered brute force. The figure's erect attitude, the whole weight of the body falling on the right leg, and the free play of the bent and relaxed left leg, with the left arm resting on the hips and the right arm holding the sword as a victory trophy, is at one and the same time full of quiet concentration and nervous tension. This classical weighting according to the principle of ideal *contrapposto,* i.e. tension and relaxation (weight on one leg, none on the other) clearly goes back to Graeco-Roman models. Once this figure is understood, so is the nature of Renaissance sculpture, and Jacob Burckhardt's statement that the Renaissance was the 'discovery of the world and of Man' seems valid. From now on the naked human form, the nude, remains the governing problem in sculpture, like the central structure in Renaissance architecture.

In his two monumental free-standing pulpits on marble pillars for San Lorenzo (Plate 45) Donatello also had reference to the ancient world (or more accurately to the Early Christian-Late Classical-transition period). These are placed opposite each other and allude quite clearly to the practice in classical early Christian churches of employing double pulpits, known as 'ambos', for the separate reading of Gospel and Epistle. The large reliefs relating the story of the Passion can also be traced back to the bronze technique used in classical antiquity and inherit its formal legacy in their accompanying decorative motifs.

Another new sculptural development in Donatello's generation was the free-standing choir-loft. Medieval divine services also had choirs, of course, but the elevated platform then apparently consisted only of perishable material (probably wood), as no example has survived. In the 1430s Donatello and Luca della Robbia tackled this assignment for the Florence Cathedral in monumental fashion (Plates 46 to 49). Both artists selected rare marble as their material and Donatello, in his singing gallery (in Italian, *cantoria*) built between 1433 and 1439, introduced a whole galaxy of classical forms, with double-ringed vases, acanthus leaves, corner palmettes and a dancing row of exulting angels, the effect of which is anything but Christian and reminiscent rather of the Dionysiac transports of putti in some heathen bacchanalia (Plate 46). Luca della Robbia tackled the same assignment in the Cathedral almost at the same time, another demonstration of the Florentine principle of competition. In the group of singing boys and music-making angels (Plates 47 and 48) he combined truthfulness and nature with classical grace. The dress in particular, its transparency permitting like some Greek *peplos* a view of the classically proportioned bodies, is wholly in the classical spirit.

50 Luca della Robbia: Tomb of the Florentine Bishop Benozzo Federighi, 1455–1456. Florence. Santa Trinità. The tomb of Federighi, who died in 1450, is one of della Robbia's major works, created in 1455–1456 originally for the Florentine church of San Pancrazio but transferred here in 1896. The face of the deceased was copied from the death-mask in accordance with the Renaissance feeling for reality. The upper section of the catafalque shows Christ in bas-relief, as the Man of Sorrows, flanked by Mary and John. The genii on the plinth, bearing a laurel wreath and a commemorative inscription, are very much in the Greco-Roman manner while the glazed terracotta frieze of flowers encircling the entire tomb, a technique for which the della Robbia family was famed throughout Italy, is magnificent in its gleaming fresh colour.

R·P·
BENOTII DEFEDE
RIGIS EPI FESVLANI
QVI VIR INTEGERIMAE
VITAE SVMA CVM AVID
VIXIT·ANNO QVE
M·CCCCL·DEFVN
CTVS EST

51 Antonio Rossellino: The tomb of the Cardinal of Portugal, 1461. Florence. San Miniato al Monte. This funeral monument, which was started in 1461, incorporates a classically stylized version of the classicizing immortalization and glorification of the dead man on the 'everlasting catafalque', which is framed by a niche looking like a triumphal arch. The sarcophagus of the Cardinal Archbishop of Lisbon is copied from a classical porphyry sarcophagus that stood by the Pantheon in Rome in the fifteenth century. The mosaic floor also imitates classical models, as does the stone curtain bordering the niche.

Luca della Robbia, along with the sculptors Bernardo and Antonio Rossellino and Desiderio da Settignano, also helped to develop a new way of embellishing churches—an imposing wall tomb set in a niche. This sculptural assignment is a particularly clear illustration of the spirit of the time, and of its feeling for antiquity. Whereas medieval man had felt himself a *viator mundi,* a 'wanderer in the world', a modest pilgrim on the way to his heavenly abode, Renaisssance man regarded himself as *fabor mundi,* master, creator and ruler of 'his' world. This now found expression in the tomb-cult. The traditional form of tomb derived from the fourteenth century—a framed niche in the church wall, with the deceased lying on a bier or sarcophagus, a 'perpetuation' of the catafalque so to speak—now underwent a decisive transformation. Two good examples of this style, which evolved in Florence and soon spread all over Italy, are Luca della Robbia's tomb of Bishop B.

Federighi (deceased in 1450) in Santa Trinità (Plate 50) and Antonio Rossellino's tomb of the Titular Cardinal, Jacobus of Lusitania (Portugal) in San Miniato al Monte, dated 1461 (Plate 51). The new version emerges particularly clearly in the Rossellino tomb. The heroic feeling for life possessed by Renaissance man, who was concerned more with life on earth than with the after-life, continued to the very threshold of death. The 'eternal catafalque', occupying its own space and full of self-awareness, stands freely in a large niche, surrounded by a kind of triumphal arch. Little angels flank the corpse. they have the form and cheerfulness of classical putti. Even the remaining celestial figures in attendance scarcely exercise a Christian effect but rather resemble heathen genii. The model for the Madonna in the crowning terra cotta tondo more closely resembles a classical Athena than the Blessed Virgin. The symbol of the cross is not to be found anywhere in the monument, and the foot of the catafalque displays cornucopias, festoons of fruit and fabulous creatures from the humanist treasury. The heaven which this high prince of the church hoped to enter had probably just as much to do with the Olympus of the ancients as with the Christian beyond, and the way thither was indicated by maxims from Greek and Latin philosophy. However that may be, the 'Cardinal of Portugal' undoubtedly saw a reliable pledge of another life and of immortality for his name in his earthly memorial, expressing as it did the period's all-embracing sense of glory and its tendency to immortalize in art a person who was outstanding and render him eternal through art, in a secular kingdom of 'salvation through beauty'. Every Renaissance memorial has this ideal background, from portrait-busts of distinguished people to equestrian statues and monuments to Princes.

Michelangelo: Sculptor in Florence and Rome

It was mere chance that the greatest Florentine artist of all, Michelangelo, was not born in the city in which, apart from Rome, he worked almost exclusively. In the year of his birth, 1475, his father occupied for one year the office of mayor in Caprese (a mountain village north-west of Borgo San Sepolcro) where the *divino* first saw the light on the sixth of March. Michelangelo grew up in Florence and Settignano, where the family possessed a small property. For a brief while only he attended a Latin school and at the youthful age of thirteen was apprenticed to the important Florentine Early Renaissance painter Domenico Ghirlandaio, for three years. After just a year, however, he left the artist's studio to enter a sculptor's, possibly that of Benedetto da Maiano, in 1489. Again only a year later, his academic education and training took a turn very different from that of the usual apprentice. He became a guest in the family palace of Lorenzo the Magnificent. There he familiarized himself with the ideas and philosophy of Neo-Platonism which was studied in the circle around Lorenzo and Politian. In the classical garden of Lorenzo's villa before San Marco he studied and drew the statues and sarcophagi. After Lorenzo's death in 1492, when Michelangelo was seventeen, he returned home and it was at this time that he produced his first two works: the bas-relief of the Madonna of the Steps and the high relief of the 'Battle of the Centaurs' (Plate 54). Though the Madonna of the Steps still betrays a number of uncertain qualities, in the perspective for example (the Christ child's back, the Madonna's foot), the Blessed Virgin is nevertheless splendidly seated in flowing garments, as dignified as a Roman matron. In the 'Battle of the Centaurs' Michelangelo, with the arrogance of youth, appears to have taken delight in his own assurance in handling the chisel. Inspired by the classical sarcophagi displayed in Lorenzo's garden, but also by the pulpits of Niccolò and Giovanni Pisano, he produced the most varied views of the body in different attitudes. Frontal, rear and profile views are displayed almost with enjoyment, and even the problem that had posed difficulties for every sculptor since Phidias, representation of the centaur, i.e. the transition from horse to human, was courageously tackled by skilfully

A partly completed marble block intended to represent a giant, had

52 Andrea del Verrocchio: 'Doubting Thomas', 1481. Florence: Orsanmichele, East Side. This bronze group portraying the Resurrected Christ showing Doubting Thomas the wound in his side is one of Verrocchio's chief works and is dated 1481. The niche framework of 1422 is by Donatello. The sculpture belongs to the series of Orsanmichele niche figures of guild-saints, each of which was commissioned and handed over for safe keeping by one of the guilds. From time to time, on saints' anniversaries for example, masses financed by the guilds were conducted at portable altars in front of the various niches. In addition to the Verrocchio 'Thomas', Orsanmichele contains Donatello's 'St Peter', Nanni di Banco's 'St. Philip', Donatello's 'St. George', Ghiberti's 'St. Matthew' and 'St. Stephen', Nanni di Banco's 'St. Eloi' and Donatello's 'St. Mark', all produced at the beginning of the fifteenth century. The masterpieces assembled here make Orsanmichele one of the finest open-air museums of sculpture in the world. Orsanmichele was originally designed as a covered public market from 1337. A miracle-working image on one of the pillars became the subject of popular pilgrimage, with the result that the hall turned into a building unique for its notable combination of religious devotion and marketing.

been lying in the cathedral's building yard since 1464. Michelangelo was commissioned to complete this in the form of a colossal figure of David (Plate 56), David's victory over Goliath being regarded as the counterpart in the Old Testament of Christ's victory over Lucifer. Even in the Middle Ages it had become a political symbol of bravery and of the freedom won by the victory of the 'weak' over the 'strong'. At the behest of the Cathedral Museum and the Wool-Weavers' Guild a commission was set up in 1504 to decide on a new site. Among the members were Leonardo da Vinci, Botticelli, Filippino Lippi, Giuliano and Antonio da Sangallo. The space in front of the Palazzo Vecchio was selected, for 'just as David defended his people and led and governed with justice, so the protectors of Florence too should defend their city with courage and govern it with justice' (Vasari). Michelangelo's 'David' is the first free-standing sculpture placed on a plinth since the end of the classical era and anyone intelligently observing the 4.10 metre (13′) high statue in white marble, contrasting with the Palazzo Vecchio's warm brownish chunks of fairly rough-hewn stone (Plate 16), will willingly admit that the choice of site accorded well with the artist's intentions.

Although he was still barely thirty, Michelangelo was already enjoying the highest form of recognition in Italy, and even in France, where François I later tried in vain to acquire one of his works. That fame was to last until the artist's death and indeed was trumpeted abroad immediately afterwards louder than ever. As early as 1496 an art-dealer had sold a 'Cupid Asleep' by Michelangelo as a piece of Graeco-Roman sculpture. In 1506 the Sultan proposed that he should build a bridge over the Bosphorus, and that at a time when the artist had done little or nothing on the architectural side. When Cardinal Medici was elected Pope in 1513 as Leo X he said of Michelangelo: 'We grew up together.' 'The one who chisels as well as he paints: *Michel più che mortal Angel divin*', (More than a mortal, an Angel Divine), as Ariosto, in the thirty-third song of his *Orlando Furioso,* paraphrased Michelangelo's name in 1516. He who even in his youth had been compared to Phidias would later go so far as to assume the role of Alexander the Great's legendary architect Deinocrates, whose ambition it was to carve a statue of his king out of Mount Athos. In 1505 'Michelangelo planned to fashion a colossus out of a mountain of marble in Carrara which would be a distant landmark for soldiers' (H. Keller 1975). And in 1563, one year before his death, he was elected Head of the Florentine Academy founded by Duke Cosimo, along with the Duke himself. Giorgio Vasari's *Lives of the Most Excellent Painters, Sculptors and Architects* had appeared in Florence in 1550. This account of the lives of Italian artists dealt only with those who were deceased, with one exception: Michelangelo. Three years later came Ascanio Condivi's *Life of Michelangelo Buonarroti,* which was devoted solely to the 'Divino'.

Thanks to Vasari's portrayals, and also to numerous drawings and a lesser number of *Bozzetti* (three-dimensional models of sculptures) we know a lot about Michelangelo's working habits. Drawings were the initial preparation for a work: precisely executed studies of a leg or a head; work-sketches giving the sweeping outline of a complete figure were accompanied by exact details of the measurements, to allow assistants to rough-hew the figure from the marble; and finally full sketches showed figures for a tomb, perhaps along with the architecture, and were probably suitable for showing to patrons. Three-dimensional *bozzetti* were done at the same time, for Michelangelo could only imagine his figures in the round. Beginning with small wax or soft clay figures which were easily worked, he ended up with an original model; the inner core was lattice-work wrapped in oakum, on to which workable plaster of Paris or stucco was finally applied. Two of these original models, river-gods for the Medici Chapel, have been preserved (Florence, Accademia). It was now that the cutting of the marble block began.

Michelangelo supervised and conducted the breaking of the blocks in Carrara and Pietrasanta personally, which was hard work. Streets or even bridges often had to be expressly built for transport, and he complained of this in many a lugubrious letter.

53 Giovanni della Robbia: 'The Coronation of the Virgin', circa *1515. Florence. Ognissanti Church. Façade tympanum. This terra cotta relief constructed about 1515 was transferred from the older façade of the original Church of the Humiliati to the baroque façade of the Franciscan Church of the Order of Friars Minor (completed in 1637), which is why there is some divergence in the arrangement of the individual ceramic surfaces, and why blue tiles have had to be inserted at the edges, as our picture clearly shows. The relief-work on the tympanum is representative of the della Robbia family's abundant output, which is found all over Italy. They specialized in glazed terra cotta. The main area shows the Coronation of the Virgin surrounded by a chorus of angel musicians; and the base the half-figures of the titular saints of Ognissanti (Church of all Saints).*

POTESTAS

54

For decades he had to devote himself to two major sculpture commissions which, however, remained incomplete: the funeral-chapel of the Medici at San Lorenzo in Florence and the tomb for Pope Julius II della Rovere in Rome.

Negotiations for the Medici Chapel began about 1520. In the same year Michelangelo sent a first draft to Cardinal Giulio Medici (later Pope Clement VII). From then on until 1533, when he finally left Florence for Rome, Michelangelo worked uninterruptedly at this project, which was not however completed. A number of marble figures are missing as well as the whole of the paintwork. As seen by the spectator of to-day, however, it is one of humanity's undying works of art. (Plates 57–60). The figural groupings are linked together in an architectonic framework which is definitely Mannerist in tendency. Into the overlapping and classically architectural structure of fluted pilasters and high tripartite dark stone beams a second much-reduced arrangement is compressed. The figural groupings are sited in front of and within this structure; on the wall to the right of the altar, which is to be thought of as facing the entrance, Lorenzo de' Medici with the figures of 'Dusk' and 'Dawn' (Plates 58 and 59) at his feet; and left, Giuliano de' Medici with 'Day' and 'Night' (Plates 57 and 60). These two Medicis are in no way important members of the family but both had become Dukes: Giuliano, Duke of Nemours, and Lorenzo, Duke of Urbino. The two most outstanding

54 Michelangelo: 'The Battle of the Centaurs', 1492. Florence. Casa Buonarroti. Marble reliefs have a long and worthy tradition in Italy. Ancient triumphal arches and columnar reliefs, as well as hundreds of sarcophagi, had already inspired Italian Gothic sculptors such as Pisani, Arnolfo di Cambio and Maitani. Donatello took up the medium also, so that Michelangelo in this youthful work had a number of great predecessors to look back on. Nevertheless signs of his artistic ideals are plainly visible: joy in portraying the human body from all sides in complicated and contorted attitudes; attraction to the free-standing figure, which seems to break out of the frame; and use of the 'unfinished' technique.

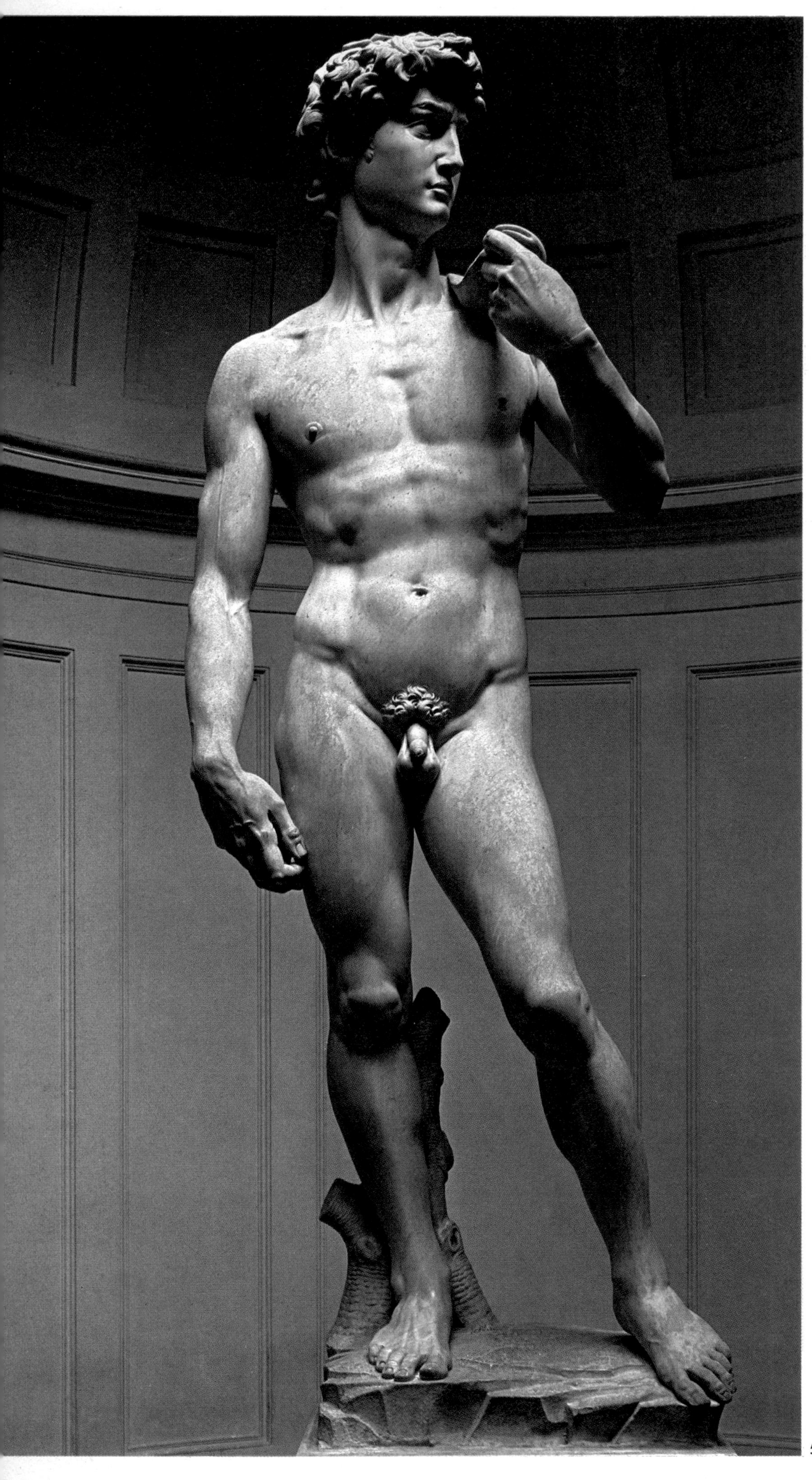

56

Previous page:
55 Michelangelo: 'Pietà', 1498–1499. Height: 1.71 metres (5′ 6″) Rome. St. Peter's. This, the earliest of Michelangelo's 'Pietàs', was commissioned by the French Cardinal Jean Bilhères de Lagraulas. The medium-sized group is to-day to be found—rather too high up unfortunately—in the first of the North-East side-chapels, the Cappella della Pietà. The harmony of this genuinely High Renaissance sculpture is revealed not only in the balance and identification of Mother and Son, beyond earthly suffering, but also in the perfect technique employed in the handling of the gleaming white Carrara marble. It is the only work signed by Michelangelo. The ribbon crossing the Madonna's breast is inscribed: 'Michelangelus Buonarotus Florentin[us] faciebat.'

56 Michelangelo: 'David', 1501–1504. Florence, Academy. The external measurements alone of this 'Statue to Liberty', which is indeed what it was intended to be, and which one has to imagine in its original setting before the Palazzo Vecchio (c.f. Plate 16), make it a matter of astonishment that this youthful work should have become such a perfect masterpiece. The 'spoiled' block, which nobody dared to work, had a base only 38 centimetres (15″) deep and 44 centimetres ($17\frac{1}{4}$″) wide, for a height of over 4 metres (13′). Michelangelo therefore had to attempt to give the figure the required expansion through twisting (turning of the longitudinal axis) and extremely skilful design.

members of the family, Lorenzo Magnifico and his brother Giuliano, murdered in the Pazzi conspiracy, were to rest in two adjacent sarcophagi at the Madonna's feet.

The need to balance the two times of day on the volutes of the high sarcophagi covers would have been reduced by the river-gods lying on the ground; and the vacant intervening space would have been bridged over so that the whole scene approached the classical High Renaissance ideal more closely. The Dukes are clad in the close-fitting leather mail of the Roman general. 'Their theme is inner mobility with exterior calm.' (H. von Einem, 1959). Lorenzo is usually nicknamed *Il Pensieroso* (the Thinker) on account of the fact that his head is resting on his hand, whereas Giuliano is called *La vigilanza* (The Wakeful), his face open and the field-marshal's baton on his knees. Both sedentary motifs express a rest that is everlasting, while the 'inner mobility' appears to break through the architectonic framework. *Dawn* and *Twilight* (Plates 58 and 59) present themselves totally to the visitor. *Twilight* in his looseness of limb seems to be already sunken in expectation of the night. 'Dawn', tense, resilient, and turned towards the work of the day, still has her head veiled in night.

The sacred Pietà theme, an image of the Blessed Virgin with the dead body of Christ in her lap, had been a widespread one in the countries north of the Alps in countless stone, wood or clay figural groupings ever since the fourteenth century. It was left to Michelangelo to introduce it into Italian sculpture with an early work, the 'Pietà of St. Peter's' (Plate 55), and three large late Pietàs, the 'Pietà' in the Cathedral at Florence (Plate 62), the 'Palestrina Pietà' in the Academy, Florence (Plate 63), and the unfinished 'Pietà Rondanini' in the Castello Sforzesco in Milan, on which he was working up to a few days before his death.

Michelangelo received his commission for the 'Pietà of St. Peter's' in 1498 from the French Cardinal Jean Bilhères de Lagraulas, who probably wanted the 'Vesper Figure' for his own tomb, as was the French custom. 'The young sculptor thus found himself facing the task of making a three-dimensional marble group, offering several aspects, out of a Gothic image which had no depth and was on one plane.' (H. Keller 1966). Iconographically, too. Michelangelo took completely new paths. Mary is no longer the careworn mother of a thirty-three-year-old son but a still girlish and beautiful woman—possibly a reference to the Virgin Birth—whose grief is barely perceptible. Nor do the features and body of Our Lord betray anything of the agony that has gone before. The wound in the side and the marks of the nails are scarcely indicated. He rests in all his beauty like a figure from the ancient world, with a sensitive yet well-formed body. The 'Pietà of St. Peter's' is a typical work of the High Renaissance which could on no account permit the degradation of the human being however lofty the end. This group is also the only work signed (on the ribbon over the Madonna's breast) by Michelangelo, as well as the only one polished throughout to a high brilliance.

Of the late Pietà groups the one in the Cathedral at Florence is the earliest, dating probably to a little before 1550 (Plate 62). This group has also been enlarged by the figures of the sorrowing Mary Magdalene and Nicodemus, and is much more vertical in structure. Christ's body is almost upright and dominated by the expressive form of Nicodemus. So deep are the feelings involved that the spiritual meaning can only be guessed at, for example from the way in which the Blessed Virgin presses her cheek ardently against her Son's. The work also remained unfinished because Michelangelo had 'spoiled' it. The left leg of the Christ figure, draped over the Madonna's upper thigh, broke off in the course of the work. Pupils undertook restoration, but not always as Michelangelo wished. The work was intended for the artist's tomb in Rome's Santa Maria Maggiore. For this reason the splendidly-worked features of Nicodemus, controlled in their grief, are thought to be a self-portrait of Michelangelo, an assumption which is totally convincing.

Pope Julius II della Rovere was one of the most outstanding and interesting personalities in the Holy See. With Leo X Medici he was in any case *the*

Renaissance Pope. He commissioned Bramante to rebuild St. Peter's; Raphael to paint the Vatican *Stanze* and Loggias; and Michelangelo to paint the Sistine Chapel ceiling. But even before he undertook these projects he was thinking, like a true man of the Renaissance, of his own posthumous fame. Fifteen months after he had become Supreme Pontiff in March 1505, he summoned Michelangelo to Rome. In the choir of the church to be erected by Bramante he was to build for the Pope a monumental free-standing tomb, conceived in the most 'hybrid' way, with numerous figures. Thereafter the artist spent forty years on the project, the dimensions of which were steadily reduced. He went to Carrara for eight months to excavate marble for the tomb, but only five months after his return misunderstandings and quarrels with the Pope led to Michelangelo's sulky withdrawal to Florence. In the end he and Julius II were reconciled and he was recalled to Rome, this time with a commission to paint the Sistine Chapel. Julius died in 1513 and his executors concluded with Michelangelo a contract for Julius' tomb, which this time would be a wall tomb.

The work, to which Michelangelo had allotted seven weeks, kept undergoing delays. In the decades that followed two Medici, Leo X and Clement VII, became Popes and pressed for the completion of their own funeral-chapels in Florence. The tomb was finally completed in 1545, with the number of figures again reduced, and was installed in San Pietro in Vincoli, where Julius had been Cardinal before becoming Pope. Only the two female figures of 'Leah', representing the *vita activa,* and 'Rachel', as an allegory of the *vita contemplativa,* plus the powerful (2.35 metres (7′ 8″) high) figures of 'Moses' (Plates 64 and 65) with the menacing Old Testament head 'sparkling with inner fire' (H. von Einem 1959), are actually by Michelangelo. A few figures have still survived, however, from the second version, partly unfinished. Among these are the two 'Slaves' in the Louvre, the four unfinished 'Boboli Slaves' (formerly built as Atlantes into the grotto of the Boboli Gardens in Florence and now in the Academy) and finally one of the Virtues trampling Vice into the dust, 'Victory' (Florence, Palazzo Vecchio, Plate 61). This marble group (2.6 metres (8′ 6″) high), has clearly Mannerist tendencies, which is rare in Michelangelo's sculptures. The slender, elongated figure twists and turns so subtly that we are constantly being offered a different viewpoint. The bent right arm and the left leg, which is thrusting the figure of Vice to the ground, are symmetrically arranged so as to balance the figure.

Observing Michelangelo's sculpture we constantly come up against something uncompleted, or sections that have been only roughly treated and 'remain in the raw'. Certainly these can often be written off as unfinished or abandoned, none too surprisingly if we follow the vicissitudes of the great projects for the Medici Chapel and the tomb of Julius. But Michelangelo made deliberate use of this stylistic approach in one of his earliest works, 'the 'Battle of the Centaurs', in order to achieve greater depth in the relief-work. Is it certain that the roughly worked head of 'Day' in the Medici Chapel was really to be given further treatment? Or does its unfinished state not convey precisely that though the body is ready for the daily chores the spirit still lingers in the twilight of night? Should we not rather, in this and many other sculptures, accept a certain 'deliberate style', i.e. the *stilo nonfinito*? There can never be a clear and full explanation, but it is certain that Michelangelo's contemporaries, Vasari above all, wanted it recognized as deliberate, and that his pupils imitated it, especially in Mannerism. *Nonfinito* became a catchphrase in the art-world, even in the High Baroque period, where the approach was widely adopted in architecture.

The genius of even so transcendent an artist as Michelangelo may wait on a favourable opportunity to bear fruit. We may ask ourselves whether creations such as the sarcophagus sculptures of 'Day' and 'Night' in the new Sacristy of San Lorenzo in Florence (Plate 60) would ever have left Michelangelo's studio had not Cardinal Giuliano de' Medici, later to become Pope Clement VII, taken it into his head in 1519 to have a monumental burial chamber

57 Florence: San Lorenzo, Medici Chapel. A view of the entrance side with the Madonna and Medici saints Cosmas and Damian (the group was originally intended to be an architectonic unit) and the figures of Giuliano de' Medici, and Michelangelo's 'Day' and 'Night' (left). The need to balance the sculptures on the cover of the sarcophagus, in the absence of the counterweight provided by the river-gods planned for the floor, is quite evident from this photograph.

57

Following pages:
58, 59 Michelangelo: 'Twilight' and 'Dawn' 1520–1534. Florence. San Lorenzo. Medici Chapel. Though the head of 'Twilight' (plate 58) is rough in outline only, the features clearly reveal a tired lassitude which is not without a feeling of contentment, as if a period of rest and relaxation had followed the day's work. The careworn features of 'Dawn' on the other hand (Plate 59) betray the anxious expectation accompanying the morning of a new day, when we do not know what it will bring.

constructed by the leading artist in the city and of the day, for Lorenzo 'il Magnifico' and other members of the family; or if Michelangelo would ever have had a chance to show his conception of the founder of monotheism had the opportunity not offered itself in the figure of Moses for Pope Julius' Roman tomb. Quite conceivably the world in that case would have lost what is most certainly Michelangelo's most famous work (Plates 64 and 65), whose *terribilità* (terrifying aspect) is attested to even in the sixteenth century, so sublime was the impact of Moses on Michelangelo's contemporaries. The question is a rhetorical one, unanswerable in effect. There can be no doubt that had their *coup d'état* against the Medici in 1440 not been so amateurishly bungled, the Albizzi and the Pazzi too—had the 1478 murder in the Cathedral

58

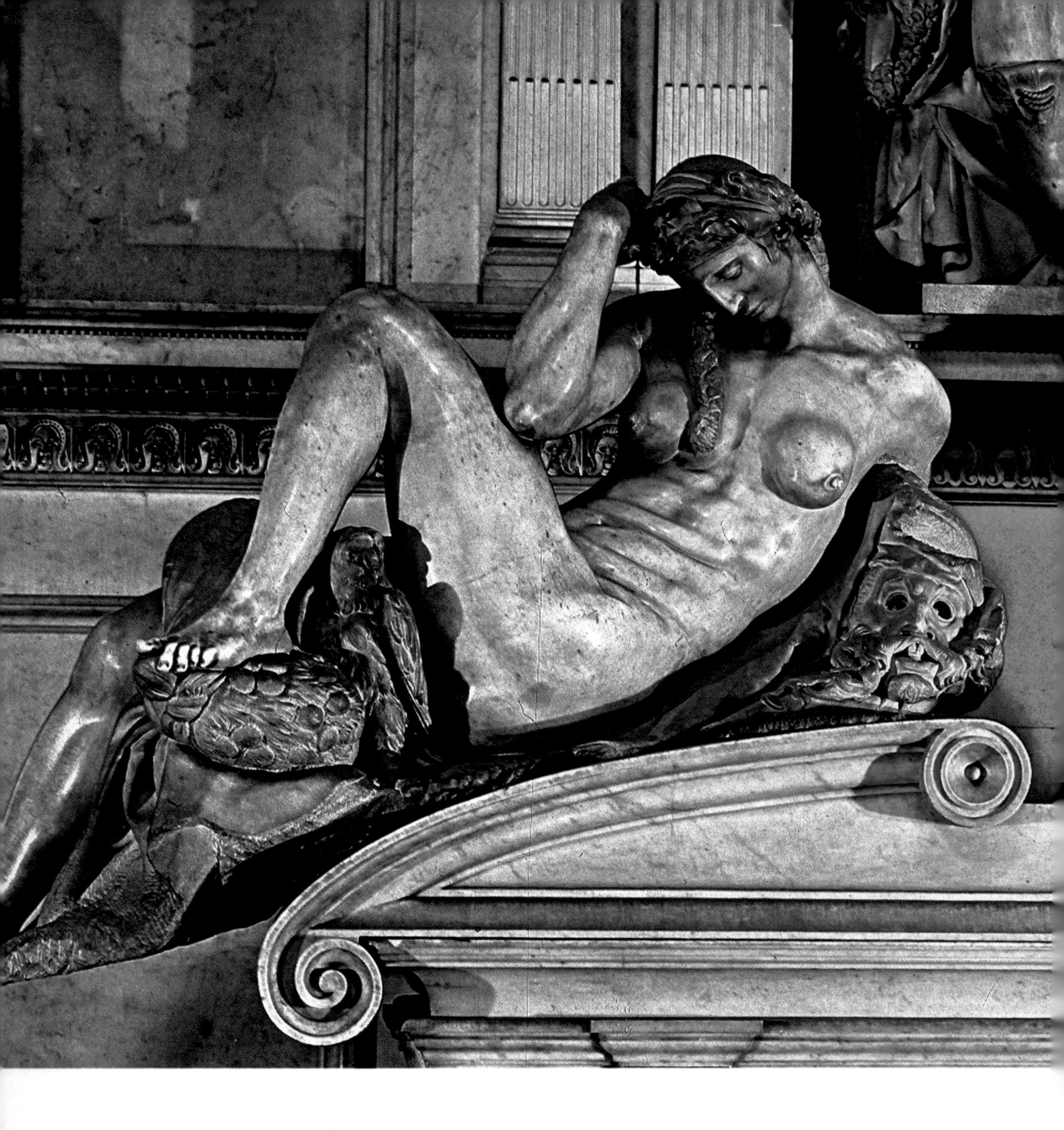

become a double murder by including Lorenzo the Magnificent—would also have promoted 'their own' artists and had 'their own' monuments erected, thus turning Florence into a hall of fame of their own. And certainly the names of the bankers who at a precise moment in the history of Early Florentine capitalism determined policy, i.e. economic policy, could easily have been changed.

From 1434 onwards, however, the municipal history of Florence is identified with the history of the Medici family, and art-history is obliged to discuss the way in which Florence increasingly became for the Medicis one great 'Hall of Fame'. After the popular movement of the *ciompi,* the

60 Michelangelo: 'Night' and 'Day', 1520–1534. Florence. San Lorenzo: Medici Chapel. The homogeneous character of the two companion figures becomes evident, particularly in their attitudes. To some extent it is a question of a classical contrapposto *design, distributed of course over two figures: a frontal view of 'Night', with right arm outstretched and left leg curved high up; and the same position for 'Day', but as a rear view. The attitude of head and arm in both also corresponds to the principles of contrapposto.*

60

'proletariat' not organized in guilds, had culminated in a bloody revolt in 1378, one of the last painful consequences of the social conflicts of the Late Middle Ages, and certain formal rights at least had been conceded to the workers, succeeding generations saw more and more power concentrated in the hands of the 'Magnates', or 'Optimates', as the refined humanistically-educated gentlemen called themselves, referring back to Ancient Rome. The Optimates, however, were identical with the great banking houses. A mercantile sense, ruthless communal policy and intelligence then brought the Medicis to the top of an internally-complicated party scene. Cosimo de' Medici (1389–1464), Head of the House and founder of the dynasty, in the end accumulated such power that he was imprisoned as a danger to the Republic and subsequently banished (1433). A year later he was back, abrogated the existing constitution, and changed the republic into a 'Signoria'. Such was the beginning of the Medici autocracy, which was to last until 1737, when the House died out. Among the serious crises were the 1440 Albizzi conspiracy, and the 1478 attempt at a *coup d'état* by the rival Pazzi, and finally the 1494 expulsion of the Medici and the interregnum of Savonarola, the censorious preacher of penitence (1452–1498), a monk whose ambition it was to set up in Florence St. Augustine's 'Kingdom of Heaven on Earth', and to purify the people through strict rules of morality and order. His anger was directed chiefly against the 'devil's work' he saw in art. Only pious imagery was permitted. Before long the most splendid paintings, sculptures and manuscripts were being burnt on great pyres in the city, among them even irreplaceable treasures by Botticelli, which Savonarola regarded as corrupt. But the spectre of this theocratic democracy, a political utopia as unfortunate and anachronistic as it was grandiose, was soon over and Savonarola himself, condemned as a heretic, perished at the stake in 1498.

The colossal upsurge of the arts in Florence around 1500 was indissolubly linked with the rise of the House of Medici, as was its ultimate decline. Following a renewed expulsion of the Medici from the city in 1527, Duke Cosimo I assumed power in 1537, when the government was transformed into a hereditary dynasty and the last democratic rights were extinguished. Art in Florence now became 'Court art' and many artists left the city, alienated by the Medici claim to omnipotence, and attracted by the freer air of Rome. In 1555 Cosimo I finally succeeded in defeating Siena and in extending his nominal sway throughout Tuscany. This was legalized by Pope Pius V, on Cosimo's appointment as Grand Duke.

From then on the history of the arts in Florence, like that of the Medici, is one of an agonizingly slow decline. Its élan grew weaker with the degeneration of the Medici dynasty, so that from 1533 or thereabouts, when Michelangelo finally moved to Rome, Florence's role in art was in the main played out. All that remained was to preserve and record. Significantly, museums were built, like the Uffizi or the Pitti Palace. Florence's contribution to European baroque can be left unmentioned. Jacob Burckhardt rightly accorded it only a few lines. The Uffizi Gallery's name derives from *ufficio,* office. It was originally conceived as an administrative centre for the politics and business affairs of the House of Medici. It included administration of the arts when creative energy subsided towards the end of the sixteenth century. It was no coincidence that the Uffizi was launched in 1560 by Georgio Vasari (1511–1574). Though an indifferent artist, he was a great critic and theorist and therefore one of the leading museum officials. In 1580 the Uffizi was wound up, with the incorporation of the Loggia dei Lanzi. Under Grand Duke Francesco I, son of Cosimo, the upper floor was rebuilt, the rebuilt section housing from the beginning the splendid Medici art collections. At the same time artists' studios and dwellings were installed. The results of this 'organization' of artistic activity into an almost business framework within the Medici bureaucracy were not impressive. The last of the Medicis, Gian Gastone, died in 1737, leaving no descendants. The city became impoverished, churches and monasteries decayed, private collectors had to live by selling off their treasures and Florence became one great antique shop.

In 1801 Napoleon created the synthetic 'Kingdom of Etruria', which in 1809 was once more transformed, with Florence, into a Grand Duchy. At the time of the Risorgimento and national unification, Florence temporarily became the seat of Italian government (1865), but soon had to surrender the function of Italian capital to Rome, which had finally relinquished that rank over three hundred years previously, at about the time when Michelangelo turned his back on it.

61 Michelangelo: 'Victory', 1532–1534. Height: 2.61 metres (8′ 5″). Florence. Palazzo Vecchio. This is the only piece of sculpture actually executed from among the six groups of 'Virtues' overthrowing 'Vices', which were planned for the tomb of Julius II. Michelangelo here demonstrates in a most elegant and instructive fashion his supreme skill and mastery in handling human anatomy. Its ability to be viewed from many sides makes 'Victory' a definitely Mannerist work.

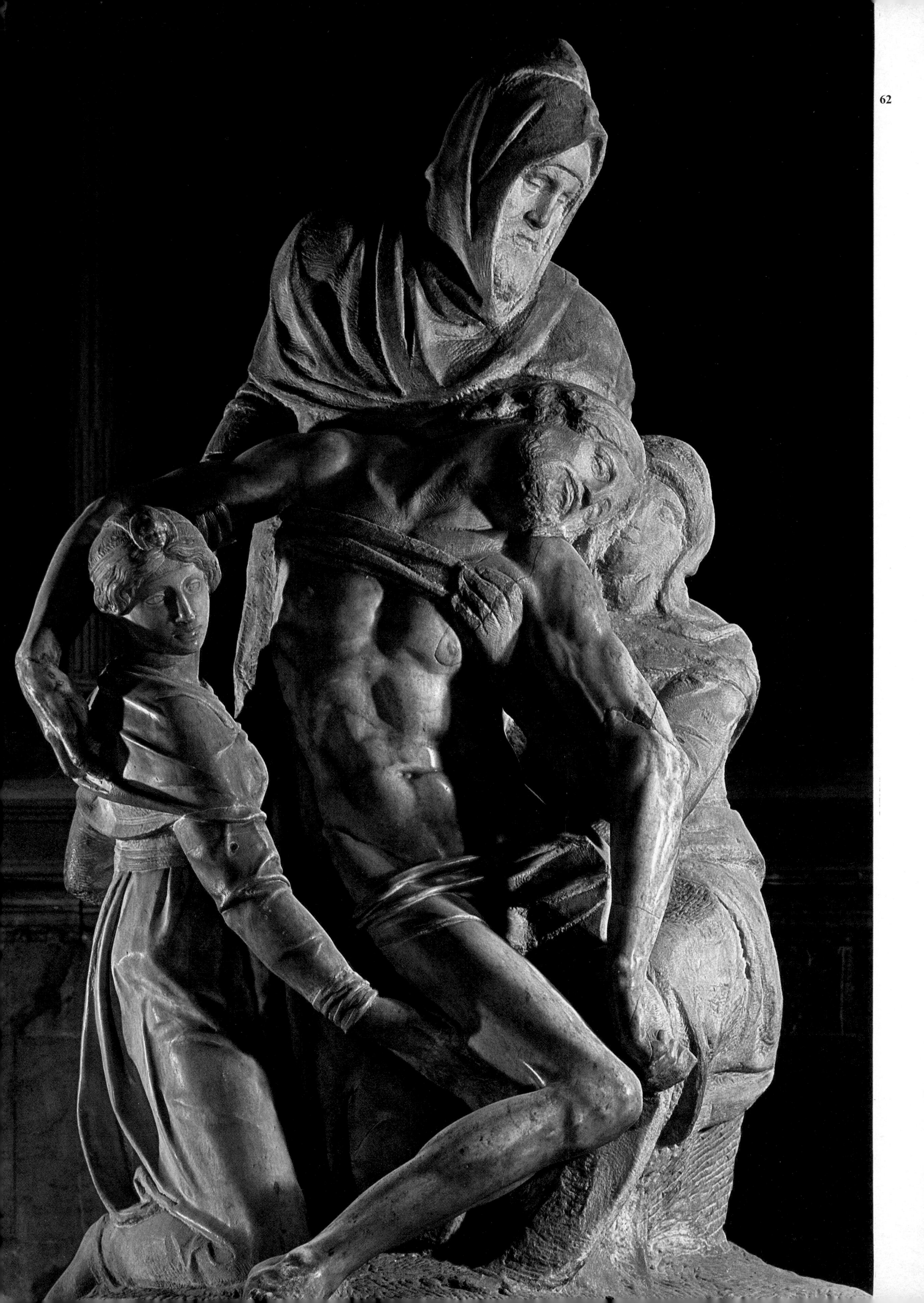

64

Page 101:
63 Michelangelo: 'The Palestrina Pieta', circa *1556. Florence. Academy. The third in the series of late Pietà groups by Michelangelo was in Palestrina near Rome until 1939. Chiselled from an ancient block of marble, the remains of an architrave can be recognised on the back. The Palestrina Pietà comes between the two other illustrations. By comparison with the frontally outspread, athletic body of Christ—a 'lame giant'—The Blessed Virgin and the favourite disciple, John, appear as incidental, marginal figures.*

Page 100
62 Michelangelo: 'Pietà', circa *1550. Height: 2.26 metres (7′ 6″). This Pietà group, extended to include Mary Magdalene and Nicodemus, was begun by Michelangelo about 1550, since it is mentioned in the first edition of Vasari's* Lives, *but was not completed, as being 'spoiled'. The left leg of the Christ figure broke during the work. The supplementary and restoration work was undertaken by Michelangelo's pupil, Tiberio Calcagni. Originally it had been intended for Michelangelo's own tomb in Santa Maria Maggiore in Rome. Despite its unfinished and badly restored condition it remains a piece of sculpture which attracts the observer by its profound earnestness.*

*64 Michelangelo and others: 'The Tomb of Julius II'. Installed 1542. Rome. San Pietro in Vincoli. What remained of the prodigious project for the tomb of Julius II was assembled here in 1542. Only the lower figures are by Michelangelo: the calm and introspective figures of Rachel and Leah (*vita contemplativa *and* vita activa*) were created only in 1542 and the figure of Moses executed as early as 1513–1516. The architectural framework, at once too rich and too subdivided, dates from 1505 and 1513–1514 (later version here). Moses was originally conceived of as a freely-seated corner figure in the upper row. The frontal view of to-day does not therefore correspond with the figure's composition and is also too low and confined. The upper section contains the Pope, resting on his sarcophagus, with the Madonna above him, and on each side a Sibyl and a prophet, all executed by pupils from Michelangelo's circle.*

65 Michelangelo: 'Moses', installed 1542. Rome. San Pietro in Vincoli. Tomb of Julius II. Of the few completed figures for the tomb of Julius II, that of Moses is certainly the most powerful. Here is the menacing leader of his people, just down from Mount Sinai, bringing the Ten Commandments recorded in the Tables of the Law, on which his right hand rests. The figure is full of urgent action, and seems to break out of the niche.

Page 104
66 Benvenuto Cellini: 'Perseus with the Head of the Medusa', 1533. Florence. Loggia dei Lanzi. Cellini's bronze figure of Perseus, dated 1533, is a masterpiece of Florentine Mannerism. It was destined from the outset for installation in the Loggia dei Lanzi, a Hall of Honour and Ceremonial (1374–1381) by the Palazzo Vecchio, which even to-day, as on St. John's Day for example (June 24) is lavishly decorated with carpets and hung with flowers. (The name 'dei Lanzi' comes from Duke Cosimo I's bodyguard, whose lancers (mounted troopers) were quartered here).

66

Rome

After his hurried journey through Italy in the autumn of 1786, eyes bent on the great goal, Goethe noted in his diary on the day he arrived in Rome (1 November): 'Well, at last I have arrived in the capital of the world!' A few days later, when the flood of initial impressions had abated somewhat, he entered the following observations under November 5: 'Traces are to be found of a splendour and a destruction that surpass anything we can conceive of. What the barbarians left has been laid waste by the architects of the new Rome. When you look at a way of life like this, two thousand years old and more, so diverse and fundamentally transformed by the flux of time and yet the identical soil, the identical hill, yes, even the same walls and columns, and hints of the ancient character still in the people, you share in the great decrees of destiny, and so it grows difficult at the very outset for the observer to

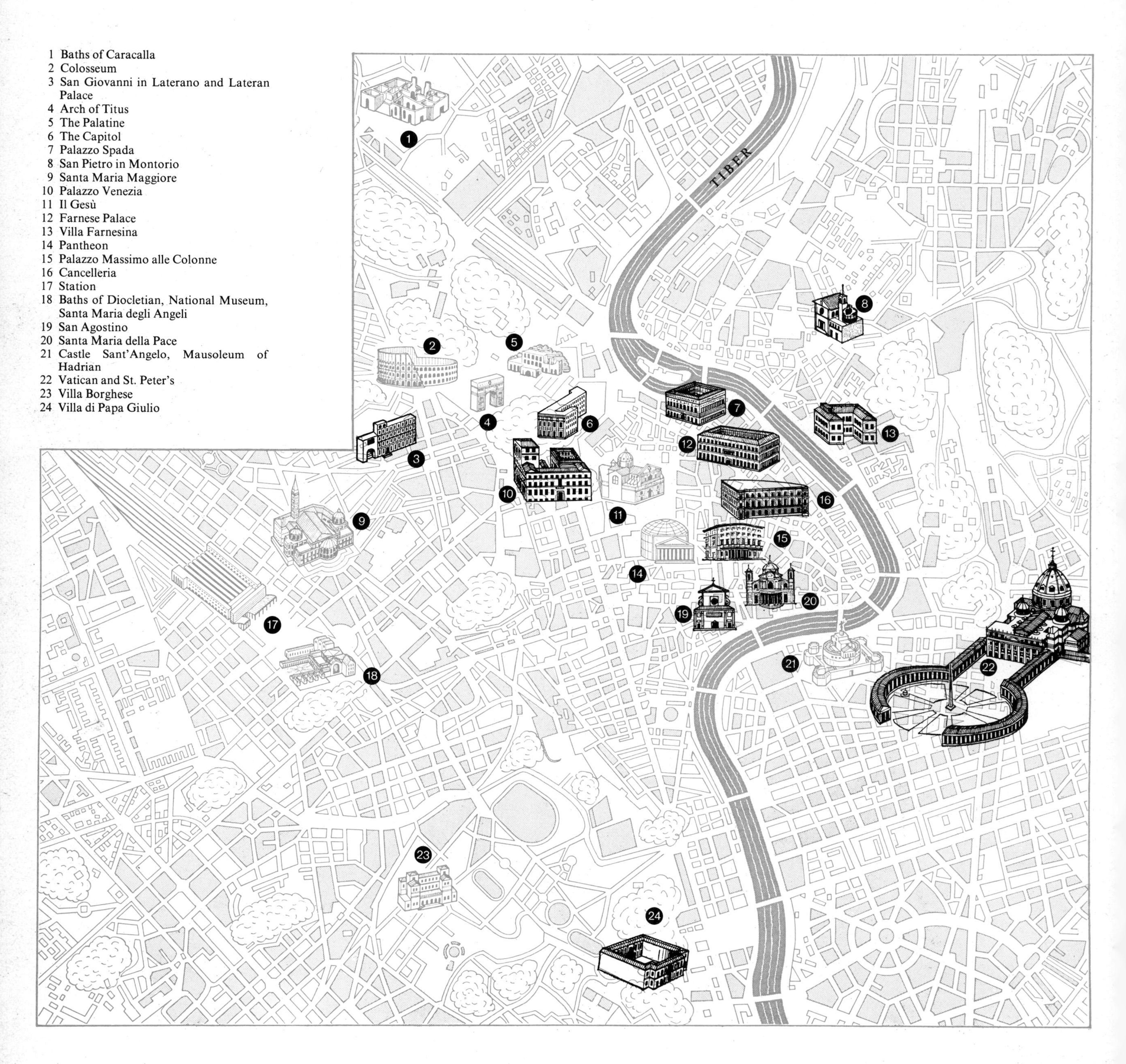

1 Baths of Caracalla
2 Colosseum
3 San Giovanni in Laterano and Lateran Palace
4 Arch of Titus
5 The Palatine
6 The Capitol
7 Palazzo Spada
8 San Pietro in Montorio
9 Santa Maria Maggiore
10 Palazzo Venezia
11 Il Gesù
12 Farnese Palace
13 Villa Farnesina
14 Pantheon
15 Palazzo Massimo alle Colonne
16 Cancelleria
17 Station
18 Baths of Diocletian, National Museum, Santa Maria degli Angeli
19 San Agostino
20 Santa Maria della Pace
21 Castle Sant'Angelo, Mausoleum of Hadrian
22 Vatican and St. Peter's
23 Villa Borghese
24 Villa di Papa Giulio

unravel how Rome succeeds Rome, not just how the new succeeds the old, but how the various eras of the old and new themselves succeed one another.'

The classical genius of the city had such an effect on the German poet, whom it had totally transformed, that twenty-eight years later, in May 1814, he could still confide to his friend, Chancellor von Müller, how he longed for Rome. Von Müller reports: 'Suddenly he stopped musingly in front of that picture of Rome and pointed to Ponte Molle which you cross, coming from the North, into the Eternal City. "I don't mind confessing to you," he said, "That I've never had a really happy day since I crossed the Ponte Molle on the way home."'

To-day it is just as hard to abandon the magic of that city landscape, its great historical memories and the eloquent testimony of its monuments as it was in Goethe's time, and the twenty-seven centuries that have passed since the ancient Romans entered history constitute through their remains a challenge to the penetration and capacity to experience and absorb of even the modern art tourist, fully equipped with reliable guide-books and plans of the city. This volume, with its twenty-five or so illustrations coming under the general theme of the Renaissance, can provide only a modest survey covering some two hundred years out of close on three thousand. The earliest monument is the Palazzo Venezia, built in 1451. Its towers and battlements still remind one of the Middle Ages, while its inner courtyard and lay-out signify the coming of Early Renaissance architecture to Rome. (Plate 67). Our series of illustrations ends, in time, with the Bernini-designed St. Peter's Square and the famous St. Peter's Colonnade, which emerged from the building-pit between 1656 and 1667 and introduces a new chapter, the Rome of High Baroque, which falls outside our province.

History

Rome's universal importance was a solid proverbial concept even for those living in the ancient world. 'All roads lead to Rome', the saying went; and '*Roma caput mundi*', 'Rome is the capital of the world'. Apart from brief interruptions this had always been accepted, ever since the Latin people of shepherds and peasants and its Etruscan kings had set out in historically early times in the Alban and Sabine Hills and in the lower reaches of the Tiber to impress their name upon the world. Rome was the world capital after the defeat of Carthage, and its sway later extended to Greece and the Near East, for the *Orbis Romanus*, the Ancient World, was identical with the *Imperium Romanum*: the Mediterranean Basin *was* the ancient 'world'.

In the High Middle Ages and Renaissance, before Italy was consolidated into a united national state, Rome was capital of the most powerful Italian autocracy, the Patrimonium Petri or Papal State; and in the quarrel between Pope and Emperor during the High Middle Ages the European world looked, as the ancient world once had, to Rome, this time as the centre of Christendom. To-day Rome with its majestic setting pulsates with life as the capital of the (comparatively young) Italian nation; and with the Città del Vaticano, the Vatican City, it is at the same time the 'ideal', spiritual capital of the most far-flung and numerically important religious community in the world, Catholicism, which has seven hundred and ten million believers in Europe, Africa, Asia, America and Australia.

Rome to-day has over two million inhabitants, and is thus the most populous city in the Mediterranean. In the ancient world the *Città eterna,* the Eternal City, was the most populous city in the world: 'the magnetic and creative centre of Mediterranean cultures' (A. Henze, 1962). Ancient Rome's eternal character revealed itself not only in its continued rise within the ancient world over a period of more than seven hundred years, but again when it survived the decline of that epoch, and once more stepped to the forefront of the post-classical Christian era, with the Apostles Peter and Paul. In the High Renaissance, and especially in the Baroque period, Rome finally became the focal point of European art and culture and was to remain so for

67

Italian and classically-minded aesthetes up to the eighteenth century and the period of Goethe. Most of his educated contemporaries in the Late Baroque era must have shared Goethe's views of Rome as the undisputed 'Capital of the World'. How did it all start?

According to modern archaeologists Rome began as a Latin village on the Palatine Hill in the tenth century B.C. The remainder of this hill has been excavated. In the eighth century B.C. settlements of Sabine farmers, shepherds and fishermen were established in defensive positions on the Esquiline and Quirinal. Mythology links the foundation of a township to the story of the twin demi-gods Romulus and Remus, issue of a love-affair between Mars and a queen's daughter named Rhea Silvia, who were abandoned on the Tiber by her great-uncle and suckled by the she-wolf on the Capitoline. Exactly what palace intrigue in which royal court gave rise to this story can no longer be discovered. In any case Romulus's origins seemed aristocratic enough to classical Romans to raise him to the status of city-founder. With their preference for precision, to say nothing of their artless manipulation of history, the Romans named the exact day and year when the

67 Rome: Palazzo Venezia. This palace was begun after 1451 by the Venetian Cardinal Pietro Barbo in the grounds of his titular church, San Marco. However much this, the earliest of Roman Renaissance palaces, with its battlemented cornice and tower, may seem to owe to the defensive palaces of the Middle Ages, the greater number of windows and especially the wide open Loggia point to the beginning of the Renaissance.

68 Rome: The Franciscan church of San Pietro in Montorio. The Tempietto in the monastery courtyard. Legend has it that the round temple built by Bramante in 1502 marks the spot where St. Peter was crucified. The purely circular central structure expresses the perfect structure of ideal High Renaissance architecture. At the top of three concentric steps sixteen Doric columns surround the central core, which is provided with pilasters corresponding to the columns of the ambulatory. A classical frieze with triglyphs and metopes supports the balustrade, and behind it the upper floor, which is set back, repeats the arrangement of the lower storey. The interior is of no artistic importance, the oustanding feature being the three-dimensional structure of the exterior and the classical proportion of the whole building.

68

69

69 Rome: Cancelleria. Courtyard. The courtyard of the Cancelleria, which dates from after 1483, was built as a palace for Raffaele Riario, nephew of Sixtus IV, and is associated with the High Renaissance in its purest and clearest form. Two floors with delicate, elegant, beautifully proportioned pillared arcades open on to the courtyard. The same theme is taken up in the enclosed third storey, which has Corinthian pilasters set against the walls, with the windows placed between them. The charm and high architectural quality of this courtyard, which at first sight appears almost over-simple, lie in its harmonious proportions and the extremely fine and elegant treatment of the details.

city was founded: 21 April 753 B.C. Rome's first kings and the nobles certainly came from the 'Twelve Towns', the federal state of the Etruscans on its northern borders. An ironworking people, they had penetrated into Tuscany, which was rich in metals, from approximately 1000 B.C. on. The famous bronze figure of the Capitoline she-wolf with the twins (added later in the Renaissance) which embodies the founding story is a masterpiece from the period when Etruscan art was in full flower, and 'zoologically' is so close to the well-known bronze 'Chimera' of Arezzo (Florence, Archaeological Museum) that one is tempted to ascribe it to the same school of sculpture. The early Roman triad of gods, Jupiter, Mars and Virinus unmistakably points to Etruscan origins.

Other Etruscan cultural legacies to the young Roman state were the insignia worn by dignitaries, the purple-bordered toga; the official chair with its ivory decoration (*sella curulis*); and the lictors, the ushers, who carried the symbol of power over life and death, the *fasces* or bundle of rods with the axe, which was taken over by the fascists. The decline of the Etruscans was therefore quite obviously not a dramatic, violent and brief process as was once thought, but the result of prolonged cultural, political and social fusion. The Etruscan character merged throughout with the new Roman culture and became a constituent part of it, giving evidence of the power of this human type to adapt and incorporate whatever was strange and came from outside, and to create a third element out of what was native and what was borrowed.

The Capitoline Hill was the centre of the loosely associated Latin and Sabine community on the Seven Hills at the bend of the Tiber. A fortress-like system of defensive works and the supreme popular sanctuary, the Temple of Jupiter Capitolinus, were to be found here. For over 1790 years the dominant and controlling function of the 'Top Hill' remained undisputed, until Michelangelo gave Rome back its old centre in a new form around 1540 with the splendid municipal architecture that re-designed the Capitol's square by providing a Senatorial Palace, a Museum, a Palace of the *Conservatori* (Councillors), open-air steps and a classical equestrian statue of Emperor Marcus Aurelius. (Plates 72 and 73). Nor was it purely by chance that the lovely 'dead girl from the Via Appia', from whose 'rebirth' could be dated the beginning of the Renaissance in Rome, was conducted in triumphant procession, with a marked sense for the historical setting, to the Capitol on 18 April 1485 (almost 2238 years to the day after the legendary foundation of the city, on April 21st) (c.f. Page 73) to be placed on exhibition.

The Latin-Sabine 'Septimontium', the group of seven hill settlements, formed an Etruscan royal city, and as such was split up into four *regiones,* or administrative areas: the Roman Quadrata, with the four most important hills, the Palatine, Esquiline, Viminal and Quirinal. But this political unit should not be accorded too much importance, since it did not number more than a few thousand souls.

Kingly rule and with it the domination of the Etruscan nobles were finally shaken off, and the first seven kings, Romulus, Numa Pompilius, Tullus Hostilius, Ancus Marcius, Tarquinius Priscus, Servius Tullius, and Tarquinius Superbus passed into the cloudy realms of fable. The Roman Republic was founded. For this too the Imperial Roman historians have given us the exact date: the year 510 B.C. When the kings had been driven out the patrician class assumed political power, as well as the control of religion, which was inseparably bound up with it. The Roman Republic had done away with feudalism but had its own problems to face in the shape of those who were prominent and in the limelight and those who remained in the shadows. Peasants had become large landowners, shepherds uncouth cattle-dealers (the Roman word for money, *pecunia,* derives from *pecus,* cattle) and simple manual workers entrepreneurs in the metal-working 'industry'. Society began to be differentiated into 'employers' and 'employed'. The Republic—*res publica* in Latin—was torn for centuries by dissension between the 'haves' and the plebeian 'have-nots', the *terrae filii,* or orphaned 'Sons of the Land'. An attempt was made to heal this breach by an ever more-complicated and still unwritten constitution. There were the estates of the realm, the Senate; a powerful administration (Municipal Council) with judiciary (Praetors); a Financial Department (Censors); authorities maintaining order and police (Aediles); and the Higher Financial office (Quaestors). In addition, as democratic cover, a popular assembly had the privilege of being convened when the State was in danger and soldiers were required. The conflict sharpened owing to fraudulent dealings among the privileged classes, which, as everywhere, preserved their threatened privileges by breaking their word and multiplied their privileges by the same process. In 450 or thereabouts something unheard-of took place. Instead of the nobles being banished, it was the people who went into exile, though not far, to the Aventine. There came the Law of the Twelve Tables, which was laid down in bronze in the Forum. Idealist historians summed this up as the 'victory of the idea of the State over the class-concept'.

External threats—the pressure of neighbouring Latin tribes, and the city's sack by the Gauls in 390 (*Vae victis*!—'Woe to the Conquered!')—were met by paying a high ransom and erecting the first Servian Wall around the

70

70 Rome: Palazzo Farnese: The Inner Courtyard. This palace was built, from 1541 on, by Antonio Sangallo the Younger, for Pope Paul III Farnese. After his death in 1546 the work was carried on by Michelangelo. Open arcades mark out the ground-floor, with Doric half-columns set in front of the pillars—another feature borrowed from classical Rome. This arrangement is repeated in the Ionic semi-columns of the centre storey, while in the upper, Corinthian pilasters arranged in the orthodox manner complete the picture.

71 Rome: Villa Farnesina. Agostino Chigi, probably the richest banker in Rome, was interested in all the fine arts, and had this villa built between 1508 and 1511 by Baldasarre Peruzzi. The building was not acquired by the Farnese until 1580. They fitted it axially and in terms of artistic composition into their expanding domain by having it converge with the Palazzo Farnese, on the other side of the Tiber. The Farnesina can be regarded as a contribution to the development of Italian villa architecture: a two-storeyed summer-palace, with an open loggia on the ground-floor and two stepped, projecting wings, it anticipates the baroque castle-type of building by more than a hundred and fity years. The costly internal decoration by Raphael and his School of course far exceeds in quality and significance the external structure (c.f. Plates 91 and 92).

71

Seven Hills (387); they thus united the state internally. Roman politics became increasingly aggressive. The Roman policy of security and peace became identical with military policy and was to remain so until the Empire's decline and fall. The surrounding country, Latium, was subjugated as far as the eye could see from the Capitol. Etruria and Central Italy were subjugated as far as the eye could see from the advanced hill-forts. But there was always another threatening hill further off with an unknown stronghold on it. Finally it was the neighbouring sea the Romans looked over, to the coast on the far shore, which also seemed menacing. The Roman Republic had soon extended very much further than the eye could see. Hungry mouths that produced nothing themselves had to be filled: officers, front-line soldiers, government officials, priests, and politicians were expensive but indispensable luxuries that upheld the State. The land surrounding the capital was no longer the only land to feed it. Traders settled in large numbers, and soon included traders from overseas. The Roman farmers and shepherds had metaphorically beaten their ploughshares into swords, and their shepherd's crooks into lances.

A port had been established in the kingdom at Ostia, and saltworks at the mouth of the Tiber to extract salt from seawater, since it was much in demand

72

in the markets of the ancient world. Now the Romans became seafarers as well, though not particularly adept ones, and Roman warehouses began to fill up with 'colonial produce' to fill the hungry bellies of the fast-growing city. The Roman Republic came into conflict with Carthage, its commercial and maritime rival. The first State Treaties of the young Roman Republic, in 510, 348 and 306, still marked the result of negotiations. Certain Carthaginian trade-monopolies were respected by the Romans (the Western Mediterranean and Gibraltar). In return the Carthaginians refrained from interfering with the allies of Rome. Carthage and Sicily became free-trade areas. But Rome was becoming more powerful. By 270 it had secured domination of the coast in Lower Italy, opposite Carthage. The Roman State,

72, 73 Rome: Ascent to Campidoglio and Senatorial Palace, and equestrian statue of Marcus Aurelius. The broad, sloping steps leading up to the Square on the Capitol, the most prestigious of Rome's Seven Hills, were executed from a design by Michelangelo. The equestrian statue of Marcus Aurelius between the two ancient Dioscuri appears a focal point to the visitor, since he sees it set against a background of the Senatorial Palace, erected in the late sixteenth century partly on classical and medieval foundations. (Giacomo della

73

Porta, Girolamo Rainaldi). The reverse view (Plate 73) shows how magnificently centred the statue is:

Helios, the sun, in his elliptical starry galaxy, flanked by the trapezoid-shaped arrangement of the Palace of the Conservatori and Capitoline Museum buildings, which lead the eye, guided by the commanding gesture of Marcus Aurelius, over the Square and down once more into the depths of the Piazza Venezia.

subdivided, according to privilege, into citizens of Rome, citizens of communities which had Roman Law and allies, covered an area of 130,000 square kilometres (50,800 square miles) and had 292,000 full Roman citizens capable of bearing arms. What had at first been a trade war at sea, with rich prize ships being seized or fishing villages burned, grew into a life-and-death struggle. The Punic Wars began. They lasted, with interruptions, for over a century (from 264 to 146 B.C.). The Romans now had to learn to fight at sea. They invented the technique of boarding and so were able to translate the rules for land battles into a naval strategy. They adopted the principles of building warships from a five-oared Punic vessel that had been left stranded. Hannibal crossed the Alps in the snow with five hundred elephants. And in

74

the first battle of annihilation in history, at Cannae, Quintus Fabius Maximus, known as 'the Procrastinator' and military dictator of Rome, sacrificed fifty thousand Romans and the fearful cry of *Hannibal ante portas*! ('Hanibal is at the gates!') ran through the city.

The elderly Cato closed his speeches with the stubborn political slogan 'Ceterum censeo Carthaginem esse delandam': 'Furthermore I consider that Carthage must be destroyed'. In the end Rome was victorious. Scipio, who was later given the title of 'Africanus', sailed over to North Africa and routed the Carthaginians in 202. Rome had undergone critical changes in those hundred years. The inevitable result of the Punic Wars was a highly-developed military and armaments industry. The impoverished peasants

74, 75 Rome: St. Peter's: The Cupola. On Michelangelo's death in 1564 the structure had advanced as far as the tambour. The shell of the cupola was completed by Giacomo della Porta between 1588 and 1590. The cupola rests on the pillars of the crossing, which are 24 metres in diameter (78'). The circular dome tambour opens up in sixteen windows, between protruding double pilasters. Sixteen ribs matching the windows culminate in the tower, again with sixteen windows. The cupola is 42.34 metres in height (137' 7", and 119 metres (386' 8") to the top. The interstices between the arches of the crossing and the

75

cupola contain mosaic paintings of the four evangelists, while the cupola shows mosaics from drafts by Cavaliere d'Arpino representing saints, whose relics are preserved in St. Peter's, canonised Popes and others. The ring surrounding the cupola base bears a mosaic-work inscription from Matthew 16, *18–19, as the supreme authority: 'Tu es Petrus et super hanc petrum aedificabo ecclesiam meam et tibi dabo cleaves regni caelorum' (Thou art Peter and upon this rock I will build my church, and I will give to thee the Keys of Heaven).*

from devastated Lower Italy moved into the city to form an unskilled proletariat. Rome became the leading capitalist and banking centre. Immeasurable wealth was concentrated in a few hands, while a new stratum came into being below the propertyless class, that of the class without rights, the slaves. In 136, ten years after the end of the Third Punic War, they rose *en masse* in Southern Italy. The result was the first mass slaughter known to history. Twenty thousand crucified slaves lined the long, straight military and commercial Roman roads. Rome had now finally changed from an agricultural state into a highly-organized modern state of officers, officials, technocrats and business-men.

Inheriting Attalos' kingdom of Pergamon in Asia, Rome in the year 133

became the undisputed dominating power in the entire Mediterranean. Social disturbances and struggles for power between rival groups henceforth took on the character of inter-Roman civil wars and led to the Republic's downfall: the reform movement of the Gracchi and the Confederate War for greater rights, Sulla, Pompey, the 'Catiline conspiracy' and the inexorable path to power of the great Caesar (murdered in 44 B.C.), which finally, after the days of the Principality, led to the accession of the Pater Patriae, Caesar Augustus, to the leadership of Rome as Pontifex Maximus and life consul (40 B.C.–A.D. 14). Under a series of Caesars, some eminent men, others pitiful figures, some sensitive art-lovers, others uncouth military men or perverse voluptaries—one of them, Caligula, is said to have made his horse a consul—the Roman Empire enjoyed three centuries of unequalled brilliance in both the political and cultural spheres. It can only be compared with Athens in the classical era, the *grand siècle* under Louis XIV, the Hohenstaufen period or Charlemagne's empire, but it lasted longer than any of them. The entire cultural world of Europe, the Near East and North Africa was Roman. The Mediterranean peoples, who in Plato's delightful phrase sat around the sea 'like frogs round a pond', conversed in terms of Roman

76 Rome: St. Peter's: the square and the façade. Carlo Maderna had begun building the nave in 1707 and it now had to be given a façade. The fact that the central structure was surmounted by a cupola caused the architect considerable difficulties. With a width of 114.7 metres (372' 9")—because the pope required direct access to the Vatican from the entrance hall—the façade had to be kept relatively low (to a height of 45.5 metres or 147' 9"), so as not to obscure Michelangelo's dome. Maderna managed to balance his structure by using vertical articulation that stands out strongly in relief, thanks to the pilasters and columns, which are set closer together as they reach the centre. The window of the Loggia of the Benediction lies under the triangular pediment crowning the central portion. From it the pope extends his 'Urbi et Orbi' blessing, 'to the city and to the world'. Bernini's trapezoid walls in the piazza leading up to the façade, together with the broad open steps, help to prevent the façade seeming squat.

politics and culture. Rome was the leader of the world and under auspicious emperors such as the cultured, Greek-minded and much-travelled Hadrian (A.D. 117–138) or the 'Emperor of Peace', Antonius Pius (138–161) or Marcus Aurelius (161–180), the 'Philosopher king', the supreme imperial leader was a symbol and figurehead for traders and legionaries in the farthest outposts of the ever-expanding Empire. In the third century the Imperium's greatest expansion was surpassed. Significantly it was now proven soldiers from the border provinces who tried to snatch the imperial Crown (the 'Soldier-Emperors'), supported by the legions loyal to them. It testifies to the vast extent, internationalism and also the tolerance of Rome that it should be the son of an Arab Sheikh, Emperor Philip the Arabian (244–249), who celebrated the thousandth anniversary of the founding of Rome.

What had Rome to bequeath to the post-classical and Christian world after Constantine the Great received Christian baptism on his deathbed (337), and after Christianity became the official state religion (391) and all pagan cults were prohibited? Or after the Western Roman Empire had been extinguished in 476 with the deposing of Romulus Augustulus by Odoacer?

Once it had been the grandiose structure housing the Roman Empire and Roman Government, which has remained a model to the present day. We must be content with a reference to Herder, who called Rome 'the proud legislator for all nations' because of its outstanding accomplishments and its flawless legal system. On the other hand, Roman architecture and building technique, as well as Roman art's special achievements in painting, historical reliefs and decorative wall-painting and wall and floor mosaics, as in Pompeii, must be of particular interest to us, for this was the legacy taken up first and most intensively by the Renaissance. It lay all over the fields, in ruins, and was thus most easily accessible, whereas in the case of painting or sculpture, accidental discoveries (still rare) or deliberate excavations were required, which only began towards the end of the sixteenth century.

Roman architects were above all great handlers of mass and space-planners, and had a gift for large-scale technical assignments. As we have seen, the first Servian city wall was built in 387 B.C. following the Gallic invasions. This was the start of planned city building in Rome. The Via Appia became the first Roman highway around 300 B.C. and in the course of the next few centuries was linked up to a dense network of other roads all over Europe, which is still, in part, the basis of modern road-planning. At the same time, about 300 B.C., the first aqueduct was built in Rome, the Aqua Claudia, and was followed by countless others in Rome itself and in the provinces. These aqueducts, bringing cool drinking-water from regions of high precipitation in the mountains, often over more than a hundred kilometres (sixty miles or so) were so solidly constructed and so effective that in Rome, for instance, they quite sufficed up until the nineteenth century to supply a modern metropolis with drinking water, contained in baroque wells. The old Acqua Vergine behind the Villa Giulia still supplies many of the Roman wells to-day. That Rome continues to be called the 'City of a Thousand Fountains' and the 'Fountains of Rome' continue to be lauded by poets is all due to the ancient Romans. Nor was drainage neglected. The Cloaca Maxima, one of the most outstanding feats of engineering and sanitation in the ancient world, disposed of the sludgewaters and is still workable to-day. In 57 B.C. under Pompey the first big popular theatre was built of stone. A succeeding building, the late Roman Colosseum, was 'colossal' in every respect, and remained the largest stone building in the world devoted to public performances, until it was eclipsed in our own century by the Yale Stadium in the United States.

Even qualified historians are largely unaware that among Caesar's many and varied talents was a particular interest in town-planning. He did not live to see his ambitious projects realized, but they were partly carried out by Caesar Augustus. It was under the latter that Rome began to change from a city of brick to a city of marble. The transformation process reached its height after the fire of Nero in 64 A.D., the first 'scorched earth' policy in history to

77

77 Rome: General view. The Vatican Palace stretches north-east of St. Peter's (which we have to imagine underneath the illustration) on slightly rising ground as far as the antique manor of Bramante's Belvedere. In other words it corresponds in extent, inclusive of the Museums and so forth, to approximately what were the Belvedere's original terraced gardens. These of course were 'destroyed' by Sixtus V, who allowed a transverse wing for his library to be built there. A second parallel wing, known as the Braccio nuovo, *was erected under Pius VII Chiaramonti at the beginning of the nineteenth century with the co-operation of Canova, for the purpose of housing the collection of antiquities. The roof of the Sistine Chapel can be seen at the right-hand lower edge of the illustration.*

have a prior architectural plan behind it. Nero's *Domus Aurea,* Golden House, the centre of this reconstruction, was a gigantic villa-like palace area, rich in green sward, lakes and ponds.

The new building techniques, such as cast-metal and mortar-work (*opus caementicium*, hence our modern word 'cement'), shuttering, marble flagging and improved structural methods produced by new vaulting techniques, altered the face of the seven-hilled city. Symptomatic of the rapidly swelling population and the growing scarcity of land were the multi-storeyed houses that had grown up in the city centre, new in appearance and turning their façades and corridors to the street, with balaconies and columned halls, while their rear wall, which looked over a courtyard, was neglected. The town-palace architecture of the nobility took over features of the Italic country villa with garden parterres, while the Imperial fora, with their widely spaced axes, temples, staircases, columned halls and basilicas gave rise to representational pleasure grounds of monumental proportions. The Roman market basilica, a hall with several naves and heavy tunnel vaulting, earmarked for legal hearings and marketing, proved to be a future model for Christian architecture. Most of the monumental structures of the Empire period still survived in the fields of ruins, being practically indestructible—the Forum Romanum and the Palatine, the Capitol, Colosseum, Baths of Diocletian and Caracalla, Castel Sant' Angelo (Mausoleum of Hadrian), Arch of Constantine, Arch of Titus, and the Pantheon, to mention only the most important.

So far-flung were the boundaries of the ancient city that it was not until this century that modern Rome penetrated beyond the Aurelian brick wall surrounding the city, proof of the enormous area Ancient Rome covered by the standards of antiquity. With the beheading of the Apostle Paul on the road to Ostia and the crucifixion of Peter on Mons Vulcanus in the year 64, the Christian history of Rome begins, along with the history of the Popes and Bishops of Rome. Their names have come down to us, though with no very precise details because the first Popes, Linus, Anacletus, Clement, Alexander, Sixtus, Evaristus, Telesphorus and Hyginus, in the first and second centuries A.D. were the hunted ringleaders of a rebellious sect consisting of slaves, freed prisoners, foreigners and social misfits, a body that met together in secret, in the skilfully camouflaged underground premises of their cult, cellars and catacombs. Even midway through the third century cruel persecutions of the Christians took place under Decius, Valerian and Diocletian, until the Edict of Tolerance from Milan (313) brought freedom of conscience and equality for Christians. The Church of Rome was able to expand without hindrance in the Empire's last year. It sent out missionaries freely, came to an understanding as regards the legacy of classical art, culture and philosophy in such a way that—progressing via assimilation—it did not simply cast aside what was left of paganism but took it over, a principle that was to be applied again in later church history. The first Papal Palace on the Lateran emerged from a classical imperial palace, while the Lateran Baptistery was built on the foundation walls of a classical Piscina, and the Pantheon was turned into a Christian church. Rome's most important churches were built in the fourth and fifth centuries and still mark the city scene to-day. They all followed the basilica plan adopted from the time of the Empire, though for Christian purposes it was redesigned, with a commanding central nave, flat roof and apses. The imperial 'arch-basilicas' of San Giovanni in Laterano, San Paolo fuori le Mura and St. Peter's predecessor, Old St. Peter's, plus the parish-churches of Santa Maria Maggiore, San Lorenzo fuori le Mura, Santa Constanza, Santo Stefano Rotondo, San Pietro in Vincoli, San Clemente and others, belong to this group, with their splended mosaic and marble work, which is still preserved.

The fate that had been predictable since the centre of gravity shifted East and the capital of Christianity moved with Constantine to Constantinople in the year 330, took place when the great migrations began. In 410, 455 and 546 the Visigoths under Alaric, the Vandals under Gaiseric and the Ostrogoths under Totila attacked the city, plundering and carting off whatever their horses and swiftly-assembled baggage-trains could carry. The Northern cavalry enriched themselves on the bankrupt estates of the old Roman Empire, yet were unable to remove the most valuable treasure of all: the monumental fields of ruins which were falling more and more into decay, mercifully covered with humus, and as pasture-land immune to the researches of modern archaeology; or else plundered by quarry-owners and lime-burners. The population meanwhile rapidly declined. When Romulus Augustulus was deposed in 476 there were only some 25,000 left out of 750,000 to 1,500,000 inhabitants of the Imperial City.

After three hundred years of decline, the rise of the Papacy, and hence of the city itself, began about the middle of the eighth century. The outstanding and shrewd Pope Stephen II (752–757) embarked on a major political campaign. Under the protection of Pepin, King of the Franks, whom he anointed a second time in St. Denis, he beat back the threat of the Longobard King, Aistulf. Pepin and his sons thereafter styled themselves 'Patricius Romanorum', Protector of the Romans.

Pepin wrested from Aistulf the Exarchate of Ravenna and the Pentapolis (the territory of the five seaside-towns, Rimini, Pesaro, Fano, Sinigaglia and Ancona on the East coast of Italy) and presented them to the Pope (the 'Pepin Gift', 754). These, together with Rome, formed the nucleus of the later Papal Territory. Subsequently the Pope raised claims to political sovereignty independently of Eastern Rome, basing his right to autonomy on a cunningly forged document from a French monastery, the 'Gift of Constantine' according to which Constantine the Great transferred the western half of the

Following pages:
78 Rome: Vatican Library: The vaulted hall, over 70 metres (227′ 6″) in length, was erected by Domenico Fontana in 1588 on the instructions of Sixtus V and is made even more splendid by the wall frescoes. The types of decoration are reminiscent of the School of Raphael 'grotesques' in the Loggias of the Vatican and the Villa Madama. Pope Nicholas V (1447–1455), a passionate collector of books and connoisseur of literature, had laid the foundations of the Vatican Library, which Sixtus IV (1471–1484) extended. To-day, with 25,000 medieval manuscripts, 7000 incunabula, 600,000 handwritten documents and 950,000 printed works, it is regarded as the most important library in the world.

Empire to the Bishop of Rome and recognised the primacy of the Eternal City over all other churches. It is one of the ironies of history that this forgery was later unmasked within the religious circles of the Papal Roman Court. Lorenzo Valla (1405–1457), a highly-qualified philological secretary to Pope Nicholas V (1447–1455), founder of the Vatican Library, was able, by means of textual criticism, to ascribe the document to the Pepin era.

A new chapter in the history of Rome and the Papacy begins with Charlemagne's coronation by Pope Leo III in Rome at Christmas in the year 800. It became a matter of symbolic political significance for German Emperors to go to Rome for the coronation. One German Emperor, Otto II, died in Rome and was buried in Old St. Peter's (983). His successor Otto III (983–1002), a religious man and touchingly Utopian, tried to achieve his dream of a new 'Roman Empire' in Rome and resided for a time in a palace on the Aventine Hill.

But the holy alliance between the German conception of Empire, the Italian Papacy and the Eternal City remained but a dream, which disappeared in the course of conflict between the Popes and Hohenstaufen Emperors, though not without fostering Dante's Utopian vision of a 'world monarchy'.

In the Middle Ages Rome was ruled by powerful city families who were often little more than robber-knights or successful highwaymen with artificially constructed family-trees. Bloody feuds raged between them. They had settled in borrowed shells, the ruins of ancient buildings, like hermit-crabs. There were the Counts of Tusculum, the Crescenzi, the Frangipani, Pierleoni, Colonna, Orsini, Savelli and Anguillara. Fortified eyries were built in theatres, baths and stadiums into which they withdrew when fighting flared up between 'Papists' and 'Imperialists'.

But the genius of the city continued to operate unseen and the shades of the past were not completely gone. Under Arnold of Brescia in the mid-twelfth century and particularly under Cola di Rienzo in the middle of the fourteenth century the citizens of Rome tried to make the idea of a Roman City-State on the old classical model a reality. Cola di Rienzo is already a completely Renaissance figure. During the period when the Papacy was under the worst threat in its two thousand-year-old history, the exile to Avignon and the manipulation of the Pontificate by the French crown (1309–1377), this political adventurer tried to reconstruct the Roman *res publica,* by careful interpretation and implementation of historical records and practice. He banished the nobles, appointed himself to the tribune of the people (1347) and proclaimed a republic. The fact that this produced nothing but a 'marvellous comedy' (J. Burckhardt) was due to the rottenness of Italian political conditions, and not to Cola di Rienzo or to lack of interest in the national past. In 1354 Cola di Rienzo lost his life at the hands of the same 'Plebeians' whom he had tried to help to a class-consciousness of the ancient Roman type.

Meantime the population of Rome had shrivelled to a lamentable 20,000 and the buildings and town-walls of the ancient world wrapped the provincial community round like an oversized garment. But the crisis now reached its turning-point. After the years of the Great Schism (1378–1417) when the 'Rock of Christ' split into the two alternatives of Pope in Rome (Urban VI) or Pope in Avignon (Clement VII), and Christendom was about to lose its way in heresy, superstitition and witch-hunting, the root-and-branch reform movement in the church resulted in the schism being overcome and in a strengthening of the Papacy throughout the political world. The Popes now felt themselves to be sovereigns and practical politicians. After the Rienzo interlude, the energetic Cardinal Albornoz (1353–1368) won back the city for the Curia, and gave it a constitution on the ancient mode, the 'Egidian Constitutions', which lasted till 1816.

The Roman Popes of the Renaissance, who came from the most important princely families in Rome and the rest of Italy, introduced one of the most brilliant eras in the Eternal City, often compared with the flowering of Ancient Rome under Augustus. The churches' 'Babylonian Captivity' in

78

79

Avignon had produced a feeling for Court life, and the nerve to acquire the necessary financial resources. The Curia was transformed into a gigantic finance house. Everything connected with spiritual office and the salvation of the faithful cost money, a lot of money, whether it was the distribution of official positions, benefices, privileges and letters of pardon, commissions (the bestowal of office) and 'reservations' (prior 'booking' of office) or indulgences, the remission of the penitence required by the church, which could now be obtained for cash instead of via crusades and pilgrimages. Naïve religious souls like the Carmelite preacher Adamo of Genoa thundered against simony (the sale of offices). In 1494 he was found murdered in his bed. Corruption thrived, especially under Pope Sixtus IV and Innocent VIII. 'Where Sixtus had obtained money by the sale of spiritual favours and offices, Innocent and his son built up a bank of secular favours, whereby pardon could be obtained for manslaughter and murder by paying high taxes. One hundred and fifty ducats went into the Papal Treasury for every penance, and anything over, to Franceschetto. Towards the end of this Pontificate Rome

79 Rome: The Vatican Picture Gallery: Raphael Room. (Sala di Rafaello). The Raphael Room belongs in the larger context of the Vatican Collections, the basics of which were laid down in the first half of the sixteenth century when Pope Julius II installed here the Olympian Hermes of Praxiteles and the Laocoon Group, discovered in 1506. Since then around this nucleus has grown up one of the most outstanding galleries in the world, the high point of which is the Raphael Room. Ten tapestries by Pieter van Aelst, after designs by Raphael (right-hand side), are displayed here and three of Raphael's chief works as an altar-painter: left to right the 'Madonna of Foligno' (1511–1512); the 'Transfiguration of Christ', Raphael's last work (1518), completed by Giulio Romano (lower figures) (one of the world's most famous pictures, comparable in artistic rating, effect and celebrity only with Leonardo's 'Mona Lisa', his 'Last Supper' (1495–1498), Titian's 'Assumption of the Virgin' (Plate 117) or Rembrandt's 'Night Watch'); and finally Raphael's 'Coronation of the Virgin' of 1503. Within a small space the visitor can thus see a comprehensive picture of the early Roman phase of Raphael, who died early and brought to a brilliant end the High Renaissance.

was swarming with protected and unprotected murderers' (J. Burckhardt: *Art and Culture of the Renaissance in Italy*, 1860). Figures like Pope Alexander and his odious children Lucrezia and Cesare Borgia, whom historians have attempted to erase from Italian history's roll of honour as Spanish 'foreigners' (Cesare in his Spanish fashion used to slay bulls in the courtyard of his palace, in solitary rituals) were no worse than their environment. The fact that they held prominent positions has caused them to be doggedly remembered. This was the reason why certain Humanist circles in Italy and Germany were secretly anticlerical, though, be it remarked, never anti-religious or atheistic. It was also the cause of the Utopian pressure of the period for a 'New Church' and a real reformation, which assumed concrete shape in Luther, and—paradoxically enough—facilitated the continuance of the Papacy in Rome by producing the Counter-Reformation in defence.

Political and personal immorality are not always incompatible with the highest artistic taste. Thus during the Renaissance Papacy in Rome we have the spectacle of the noblest pictures being painted, the choicest sculptures being created, whilst at times only a few hundred yards away human beings were being tortured, strangled, poisoned or stabbed, and the most sacred values of Christendom hawked around with the utmost cynicism, as if in some cattle-market.

Rome experienced an upsurge in architecture. Beginning with Sixtus IV and Innocent VIII and ending with the Baroque Popes, an attempt was made by deliberate recourse to classical architecture to restore ancient Rome with its great axes of road, squares and outstanding points of reference. As elsewhere in Italy, the study of antiquity became fashionable. Flavio Biondo's descriptive text *Roma instaurata*, written towards the end of the fifteenth century, became an obligatory text, while as early as 1443 a Roman reporter was waging a campaign against the vicious habit of using ancient marble for lime-burning, 'for the newer buildings in Rome are pitiable and it is the ruins that are beautiful!' Documentary evidence to the credit of the Curia's cultural policy are the frequent Papal ordinances in the late fifteenth and throughout the sixteenth century prohibiting the destruction of ancient monuments and works of art under threat of punishment. Papal architectural policy in the city and the study of antiquity went almost hand in hand, and the best artists of the time devoted themselves to the new task of making Rome the cultural centre of the world. These included Leonardo da Vinci, who had been in Cesare Borgia's service as a military engineer in 1503, Raphael and Michelangelo.

As far back as 1373 a small obelisk had been dug up near the Pantheon. The famous 'Boy with the Thorn' was recovered in the same way about 1450, and in 1506 the 'Laocoon', followed in 1510 by the Belevedere 'Apollo'. From 1540 onwards systematic excavation work was carried out in the Baths of Caracalla, and the 'Farnese Bull' as well as the 'Farnese Hercules' were found. Next came excavations in the Baths of Constantine (from 1550), and the discovery of the two 'Dioscuri of Monte Cavallo'. 1570 or 1606 saw the 'Medici Venus' and the famous painting of the 'Aldobrandini Wedding' complete the list of findings. Even to-day thirteen ancient obelisks still adorn Rome's most important squares. They all lay in the ground till they were excavated towards the end of the sixteenth century, and included the obelisk of St. Peter, found in 1586, and three others, those of the Lateran, Santa Maria Maggiore and Piazza del Popolo, all found in 1587.

The notorious 'Sack of Rome' by an army of mercenaries belonging to Emperor Charles V (1527) occurred just when Rome was being planned anew, and so left hardly a trace in the Renaissance picture of the city. Nevertheless parts of Raphael's noted Villa Madama fell prey to it. The completion of Rome's grandiose architectural reorganization was reserved for the Early Baroque period and thus falls outside our survey. Roman art is rooted in two historical and political institutions—the Roman Empire and the Papacy. These twin roots gave out branches, clambered up each other, supported each other and eventually came together to form the trunk out of

80 Rome: The Vatican, Sistine Chapel. General View. The smooth architecture of this simple store-room was created under Sixtus IV, who consecrated the chapel in 1483. The frescoes on the long walls and the twenty-eight paintings of popes between the windows were also carried out during his Pontificate, mainly by Tuscan and Umbrian painters. The chapel owes its fame, however, chiefly to Michelangelo's frescoes in the vaulting and his 'Last Judgement' on the altar-wall. Raphael's celebrated series of tapestries (now in the Vatican Museum) executed from 1515 to 1516 served to cover the lower third of the walls. This costly décor confers on the Sistine Chapel the effect of a shrine, containing the noblest of relics. It is reserved up to the present day for the most important ecclesiastical events in the Catholic world, the election of a Pope for example.

Following pages:
81 Rome: Michelangelo's 'Last Judgement' (Detail) 1534–1541. The Vatican. Sistine Chapel. Christ judges the world. The interceding Madonna on his right is surrounded by saints, martyrs and figures from the Old Testament. We recognise Adam on the left, and on the right the equally gigantic figure of Peter with, at Christ's feet, the greatest martyr, Bartholomew, holding in his hands his skin. Christ, with a great gesture of His right hand, is dividing those far beneath him, awakened to the Last Judgement by the sound of the Last Trump, into those saved and those who are damned. The picture is an excellent illustration of the technique of the buon fresco *practised from the beginning of the fourteenth century and also by Michelangelo. Following preparatory sketches (up to original size), the draft was transferred to the ceiling or walls by the aid of finely-pierced boards, the holes in which had been powdered over with charcoal. This final draft had to be covered with fresh chalk, however, if the colours were to combine well with their background. Since any schematic 'squaring' would have rendered the work more difficult the work was done in what were known as 'daily tasks'. Only as much of the prior drawing was covered with chalk as could be painted in a day, and the outlines of the body were followed, so as to have points of reference available. These 'daily tasks' can be seen clearly in Michelangelo's 'Last Judgement'.*

which, in the High Renaissance and Baroque periods, the city's present artistic shape grew.

'Let us admit, however, that it is a sad and sorry business to pluck ancient Rome out of the new city' (Goethe *Italian Journey,* 5 November 1786). But this was a task to which every artist whose ambition it was to work in Rome had to address himself. Even if he had no desire to, this was carried out unconsciously. Those familiar with the ancient art of Greece had also to reorientate themselves in Rome. Monumentality, architectonic plans that included in their dimension mountains and valleys as contained open spaces; weighty yet broad vaulting; powerful pillars with heavy architraves over them instead of columns that were 'visible at a glance'; sculptures larger than life and free-standing, not backed by a protective architectural framework; paintings in which every figure was placed for all eternity; outside staircases; victory columns and wide triumphal arches covered all over with reliefs; the elevated *gravità romana,* the weight of Roman seriousness, does not confront only the modern visitor, but had to be assimilated by artists, with an eye that was alert and took in everything. None of them escaped these impressions. They were shaped and stamped one and all by this city's radiance, and if from now on they painted, built and sculpted 'differently', i.e. in the 'Roman' way, it was not a question of external pressure but of a humble and yet proud, of an active and conscious submission. Florence was open to every artistic personality who was free to develop his own individuality. An artist born in Venice was encouraged to remain Venetian, giving himself over to the ebb and flow of the city and to its inspiration. But Rome shaped its artists and shaped them with all the weight of its existing century-old and yet still valid traditions. Florence is the city of discovery, innovation and experiment. Venice remains in the intellectual and spiritual condition in which it always existed. Innovations come out of it of themselves, and as a matter of course. But Rome reaches *consciously* back into tradition and so finds its way to the new, which even today is still involved with the past.

Rome was never a city of young styles, of joyfully experimental or exploratory ideas, but has always been a city of maturity. Only when a style has reached full maturity has Rome solemnly and sonorously taken it up, as though in final consecration. When Brunelleschi, Donatello and Masaccio created the Renaissance in Florence almost overnight, in about 1420, the Papacy was going through a period of serious crisis. One schism followed another and every legitimate pope had to contend with several anti-popes. They seldom managed even to set foot in Rome, but lived in Florence or Bologna, or eventually in exile in Avignon. Eugenius IV (1431–1447) was the first pope who managed to return to Rome, which was by then in a state of total decay. He at once started rebuilding it; but if he was to embellish his residence he and his successor Nicholas V, another art-lover, had to send for painters and sculptors in Florence and northern Italy, as well as Venetian mosaic artists such as Gentile da Fabriano, Pisanello and Donatello. Fra Angelico started working on the former Vatican chapel of the Sacrament. Nicholas V summoned to Rome the brilliant Florentine architect Leon Battista Alberti so that he could start work on rebuilding St. Peter's. He also employed Benozzo Gozzoli, Andrea del Castagno and Piero della Francesca as painters. Under Sixtus IV della Rovere (1471–1484), Verrocchio, Ghirlandaio, Botticelli, Perugino and Pinturicchio—Florentines, Sienese and Umbrians—were working in Rome.

It was not until the eve of the High Renaissance, in 1503, that Julius II managed to make Bramante, Michelangelo and Raphael, all of whom he had brought to Rome, feel so attached to the city that they failed to return to their home towns when their commissions were completed. Instead they remained in Rome and became 'Romans', since the artistic legacy that Rome could offer now fitted in with the style and ambitions of the period. Rome therefore remained the centre of the arts and the capital of the golden age of the High Renaissance. Its supremacy lasted until the Sack of Rome in 1527, when the city was plundered and devastated by Imperial Spanish mercenaries and French troops.

Rome had thus been able, as it were, to catch up on the art of the Early Renaissance, with the help of Florentine, northern Italian and Sienese artists. The almost exclusively religious art of the Gothic and Romanesque periods had passed it by, virtually without leaving a single trace, since its centres were in Cluny and Cîteaux, in the imperial 'national art' of the great cathedrals on the Rhine (Worms, Mayence, Speyer) and in the Ile de France, the cradle of Gothic architecture ranging from Saint-Denis and Chartres to Rheims and Amiens.

Italian art had without a doubt set its face against the verticality of Gothic, to replace which other forms had been found: broadly spaced-out areas and wide arcades instead of the sharply pointed type. The cathedrals of Pisa, Florence, Siena and Orvieto are there to bear witness. The mendicant orders, Franciscans and Dominicans, had built gigantic churches everywhere that impress themselves on the city scene but Rome had remained entirely unaware of all this.

Yet on the threshold of Roman art stands one of the freeest creations in all religious art, the Early Christian basilica, which seems to hold in contempt the entire classical legacy, particularly as regards vaulting. Only a few decades separated the greatest Roman example of vaulting and cross-vaulting, the Maxentius Basilica, with its massive cross-vaults and barrel-vaulting, from the old St. Peter's Basilica with its open roof-framework which leaves all the timber raftering visible. Amid all the expensive and splendid late Empire vaulting it was the late Republican or early Empire market and courtroom basilicas, in the style of the Basilica Julia or the Basilica Aemilia on the Forum Romanum, or the Basilica Ulpia on the Trajan Forum, that served as guide in building the first church in Christendom. These were lengthy structures with a high central nave and low aisles over which galleries could be placed, with a flat, coffered roof, or open rafters, vestibule and a semi-circular apse on one of the narrow sides.

The decision to refer to secular Roman basilicas in constructing early Christian community assembly halls was logical and consistent. The function of both was to concentrate a large number of people in one spot, where either the Roman orator was speaking or the Christian priest celebrated mass. The ancient Greek or Roman temple would have been quite inappropriate as an architectural model since only the priest was allowed to approach the divinity in the inner sanctum, and the audience remained outside.

None of the early Christian basilicas in Rome had towers—the Campanili allotted them to-day all belong to the twelfth or thirteenth century—since the liturgical custom of summoning the parish to worship by means of bells came into use only in the ninth century. All of Rome's early Christian basilicas, with the exception of St. Peter's, have come down to us substantially intact. The most venerable, such as San Giovanni in Laterano or Santa Croce in Gerusalemme, were of course converted to the Baroque style in the seventeenth and eighteenth centuries. Santa Maria Maggiore, where the mosaic cycle has been fully preserved, offers the visitor the clearest picture of how it must have looked originally. Alexander VII Borgia had the finest coffered ceiling in Rome completed. Begun by Calixtus III, it is said to have been gilded with the first gold brought to Europe from America.

So much was early Christendom governed by its classical legacy in shaping the basilica that other necessary Christian religious buildings also maintained their functional purpose as conceived by pagan Roman art. Among these are the tomb structures erected over the bones of particularly pious and distinguished Christians, or martyrs. The *Tolos,* the round building, windowless but with a cupola, or in any case a central structure, was retained as a tomb not only along the Via Appia but also outside Rome. Baptisteries were also invariably erected on a central ground-plan until the High Middle Ages. Since the origin of some can be traced back indisputably to the round or elliptical Roman baths, the *caldaria* or *tepidaria* (as for example San Giovanni in Laterano), it may justifiably be assumed that the tradition of centrally-structured baptisteries is due to the fact that the ancient baths were

Previous pages:
82 Michelangelo: 'The Awakening of Adam' (1508–1512). Rome. The Vatican. Sistine Chapel. The arrangement of this scene is Michelangelo's own original conception. Adam, recumbent, lethargic, engrossed, full of the earthy heaviness of the lump of clay out of which he was formed, seems to wish for animation, though his hand droops helplessly down so that the finger of God the Father, pulsating with energy, cannot quite reach it. Yet the spark may carry over at any moment.

83 Michelangelo: 'The Eritrean Sibyl' (1508–1512). Rome. The Vatican. Sistine Chapel. Michelangelo portrayed five sibyls (ancient Greek women with the gift of prophecy) in the Sistine Chapel vaulting. Of these the Eritrean is considered to be the oldest and the most significant, since she is said to have proclaimed the doctrine that there is only one God (monotheism). While the other sibyls twist and turn in various attitudes, the Eritrean conveys a composed and relaxed impression.

83

84

converted at the beginning of Christendom into baptismal fonts.

In the Christian West secular architecture played only a subordinate role throughout the whole of the Middle Ages. In the Rome of the period it did not appear at all. In Florence, Siena, Bologna and other Italian towns the feuding nobles built impregnable fortress-like palaces with high towers. In Venice, where there were no internal feuds, elegantly decorated Gothic palaces emerged from the water. In Rome it was quite different. There the influential noble families withdrew into the solid ruins of the ancient theatres and baths.

When the Renaissance began, however, the wealth of material which ancient Rome had left behind provided the best of object lessons and was appreciated by the architectural theorists of the time as a pattern to follow. The most important of these, Leon Battista Alberti, was, with Pope Nicholas V, the first to produce a project not confined to individual building schemes but one to be thought of as a piece of comprehensive town-planning. The project to rebuild St. Peter's was combined with new building and systematic planning of the Vatican. Streets were laid out in long-range perspectives as far as Castel Sant' Angelo, the Mausoleum of Hadrian, the farthest of the walls enclosing the Vatican State. It was this thinking in terms of great axes, and the gradation and architectural conception of successive open spaces which had been learned and understood from studying imperial baths and villa designs, that provided the impetus behind the townscape of Rome which now, and in the centuries that followed, began to emerge. 'The next step giving shape to the city occurs in the High Renaissance. Under Pope Leo X two diagonally branching streets, the Via di Ripetta and the Via del Babuino, were led off the Piazza del Popolo to form, with the old central axis of the Corso, a widespread network of streets in the shape of a fan, such as the baroque period almost invariably adopted for their founding cities, from Versailles to Rastatt and Karlsruhe.' (H. Keller, 1960).

A new rearrangement, which took in the widest areas and indeed the whole of ancient Rome followed under Sixtus V (1585–1590). The Pope was not moved in this by any artistic ideas, even though the end result was a masterly achievement in municipal architecture. He was more interested in a 'vast network of streets connecting up Rome's outstanding old churches in great vistas . . . [and] indicating the points of convergence by using the obelisks about to be erected as vertices' (D. Frey, 1924). In addition to the obelisk on St. Peter's Square put up during Sixtus V's Pontificate, the obelisks in Santa Croce, before the Lateran, on the Piazza del Popolo and in front of Santa Maria Maggiore, were re-erected under him to mark the great pilgrimage roads. His favourite church, Santa Maria Maggiore, formed the centre of this network. The shaping and architectonic designing of the squares came next. St. Peter's Square, the Piazza Navona with Bernini's Fountain of the Four Rivers, the attractive Rococo square of Sant' Ignazio, Piazza Venezia and Piazza del Popolo, which found its final form only in Valadier's classicism, all belong to the Roman scene, as does the earliest square of all, the Capitol, (Plates 72 and 73).

The Capitol, the smallest of the Seven Hills, was ancient Rome's religious and political centre. The Senatorial Palace, seat of city government, dating in its present form from the sixteenth century, stands on classical and medieval foundation walls. Michelangelo was commissioned to replan the irregular square, sloping unevenly down at the sides, once the equestrian statue of Marcus Aurelius had been brought from the Lateran to the Capitol in 1538. This bronze image of the Emperor on horseback is the one and only original that has come down to us from the ancient world. Assumed to be an equestrian statue of Constantine, the first Christian Emperor, it was therefore not destroyed. Execution of Michelangelo's magnificent designs was begun only shortly before his death. First the paving of the three-stepped oval was begun. The Emperor as Helios, the Sun-God, was to be portrayed in the centre of a radiating ellipse (Plate 73). The two lateral palaces were erected only after Michelangelo's death, but in strict accordance with his plans. Here

84 Michelangelo: 'The Expulsion from Paradise'. Detail: Head of Eve. Rome. The Vatican. Sistine Chapel. The figure of Eve seems to cower, as it were, beneath the Divine wrath. Only the features appear bold and free, full of the awareness she has acquired from eating of the Tree of Knowledge.

powerful fore-pilasters combine to form an orderly system which is colossal in its effect—the first in a secular building since the ancient world—the ground-floor resting on columns and straight architrave. The broad sloping approach (Plate 72) to the square, which is not oblong but trapezoid, is also from designs by Michelangelo, while the marble figures of the Dioscuri, from the Late Empire, provide a solemn frame for the entrance 'into the Square', *in piazza*, as the Italian language attractively puts it.

'Thus regarded, Michelangelo's Capitol represents the most powerful and profound incorporation of Italian Renaissance thinking. Antiquity is the basis and centre, but also the source of spiritual renewal. Michelangelo did

85 Sandro Botticelli: 'Scenes from the Youth of Moses', 1481–1482. Rome: The Vatican, Sistine Chapel. Botticelli's fondness for story-telling, uniting several scenes in one picture as in medieval painting, gives the fresco an Early Renaissance freshness. The wealth of charming detail almost destroys the pictorial unity.

85 not imitate classical antiquity in detail. Neither the plinth, nor the oval, nor the architecture of the palaces imitate ancient forms. On this spot we feel clearly that the ancient world is over, but that through Michelangelo's interpretation of it a concept of spiritual power has been captured which we cannot escape because it has begun to operate in ourselves.' (E. Hubala, 1968). The Capitol Square is for that matter only one of many examples of the fact that in Rome sculptures, whether classical, Renaissance or Baroque, were never erected in isolation. They had always to be seen against the background of the space, the square, in short the entire architecture.

If municipal architecture and the planning of squares covered such wide areas, it is hardly surprising that the same stylistic principle should have been adhered to in building projects that were intended at the outset to incorporate free spaces and nature herself, in villas and gardens. The artistic conception of the villa, a fine example of which, next to the Vatican's Belvedere, is the unfinished Villa Madama on Monte Mario, built by Raphael, had no need to be inspired by ancient ruins. Architects like Bramante, Raphael, Vignola, Giacomo della Porta or Pirro Ligorio got their ideas from Roman writers on architecture and from Vitruvius, from whom even the great Alberti took over entire passages, and especially from the descriptions of villas by Pliny the Younger. A villa should be built on slightly rising ground, about half way up, on a *locus amoenus,* a pleasant or favourite spot, with a fine view of nature, which would then so to speak be framed by the architecture. The view, the *prospectus*, was a legally protected piece of property in ancient Rome. Any such villa also possessed spacious gardens, shady and cool, and cryptoportici let into the revetment walls of the terraces; 'subterranean' corridors open only on one side, for a cooling sojourn on a hot day; spacious baths, in most cases also semi-subterranean, and all sorts of fountains, swimming-pools and water-displays. Recently a letter of Raphael's was found, expressing his thoughts on the final shape to be given to the Villa Madama, originally built for Cardinal Giulio de Medici, later Pope Clement VII. This letter is a word-for-word quotation from a surviving letter by Pliny the Younger in which he describes his Villa Laurentium by the sea near Rome. Though today only the shell of the villa can be seen, its shape clearly shows that at the beginning of the sixteenth century Raphael intended to build in this first-century manner, including the luxurious baths that had already been laid out in the ground-floor ashlar of the villa, which was, as it were, 'kneeling' on rising ground.

If they were to be truly perfect, gardens and squares, *villegiatura* and town needed one important feature to enliven the severity of their structure and to introduce a picturesque element—water. Many poets have sung of the swishing of Rome's fountains with their waters flowing, streaming and then lying still. Indeed in the heart of the city we are, so to speak, carried along from one square to the next by the murmuring of the water. Modern Rome's plentiful water supply is another legacy from the ancient Romans, who constructed an extensive network of aqueducts to bring water from the Sabine and Alban Hills to Rome, where it ended up in the Aqua Marcia, the Aqua Tepula, the Aqua Giulia, Aqua Paolo, Aqua Felice and many others, tumbling over fountains with decorative walls and nymphs, often embellished with statues. The Popes regarded it as a point of honour to restore the water conduits and resite the fountains in even more splendid ways, and their work in this direction won them lasting fame. After supplying the Fontana della Barcaccia in the Piazza di Spagna, the aqueduct of the Acqua Vergine, which was built by Agrippa, flows into Rome's most famous High Baroque fountain, the Trevi Fountain, a high wall decorated with sculpture over which tumble masses of water. The Acqua Vergine runs with pure spring water and the modern visitor can safely drink it.

The Piazza Navona is a completely enclosed and unified square, thanks to the architecture of the walls and the three fountains, which include Gianlorenzo Bernini's Fountain of the Four Rivers. The ground plan of the square is based on an ancient stadium dating back to the time of the Emperor

86 Sandro Botticelli: 'The Temptation of Christ'. Detail. 1481–1482. Rome: The Vatican, Sistine Chapel. This detail from 'The Temptation of Christ' clearly reveals what concerned the Florentine. The entire figure of the woman carrying wood dissolves in the highly-refined interplay of line and movement, beginning with the outline of the body, then travelling over the folds in the dress, to the serpent-like curling of the hair.

86

Domitian, and was flooded on three Sundays in summer for the 'Divertimento del Lago' (Water Festival). Access roads were closed off, and the overflow from the Fountain of the Four Rivers stopped, so that the water flowed over the edge of the fountain, and the carriages of the haughty Romans rode in a 'carousel' of water.

Roman palace-building begins almost on the threshold of the High Renaissance. The Medici, Pitti, Rucellai, Strozzi and many other palaces had long since been completed, but the Roman aristocracy was still living in the ruins converted into fortresses: the Savelli in the Theatre of Marcellus, the Orsini in the Mausoleum of Augustus, the Frangipani even in the Arch of Trajan in the Forum. In fifteenth-century Florence the owners of the great palaces were rich merchants, but in Rome they were almost exclusively cardinals, though later, in the sixteenth century, bishops and officials of the Curia and even bankers ventured to build themselves palaces. Acquiring the land often proved a difficult and tedious task, but no one counted the cost and even the earliest Roman palaces were on a scale whose splendour far eclipsed that of Florentine buildings, an unconscious tribute perhaps to the *genius loci*. Certainly in addition to the desire for comfort, a thirst for celebrity played no small part among the builders: *'Elegantiae publicae et commoditati privatae'* ('The splendour of the city and the comfort of the tenants') runs an inscription on a Milan palace dating from the end of the fifteenth century. Emphasis was laid in Rome from the start on the inner 'distribution', this too being a legacy from ancient Rome, which in its baths and villas had always cultivated the utmost comfort in arrangement and luxurious furnishings. 'No such care had been lavished on entrance-halls and inner courtyards since Imperial Rome, nor on staircases since the Cretan culture, and never before on façades. Nor was comfort neglected: medium and small rooms *(studioli,* for instance) were just as expensively furnished as the reception rooms.' (C. L. Frommel, 1973). The earliest Renaissance Roman palace is the Palazzo Venezia (Plate 67), which was begun after 1451 by the Venetian Cardinal Pietro Barbo in the grounds of his titular church, San Marco. Several architects are mentioned (Alberti, Filarete, Rossellino) but none with any degree of certainty. Externally the palace and its towers are still castle-like in their emphasis on defence. But in the inner courtyard we see for the first time the columnar system preferred by the Romans from this date onwards. It can be seen here in its pure form, with colonnades on two floors and half-columns set in front.

The Cancelleria (plate 69) is generally attributed to Bramante, but the project was begun as early as 1483 and Bramante did not come to Rome until 1499. The rhythmic way in which the façade is subdivided by means of fore pilasters and the noble proportions of the three-storeyed inner courtyard clearly make the Cancelleria the perfect Roman Renaissance palace. On the other hand (plate 70) the Palazzo Farnese, which Antonio da Sangallo the Younger started building for Paul III in 1541, though the third floor in the inner courtyard was completed by Michelangelo, already appears to anticipate baroque trends, or, to put it another way, harks back once more to the classical style of ancient Rome, though much more emphatically and deliberately. This is reflected chiefly in the very deliberate distribution of the inner space, in the way the central axis opens on to the garden above the central loggia and the expensive internal decoration. With the coming of the High Renaissance the personalities of individual artists naturally began to emerge more clearly than was possible in Florence at the beginning of the fifteenth century. As a result the Roman palaces also create a far more individual impression.

For over two hundred years, however, Rome's greatest architectural project was the rebuilding of St. Peter's, including a whole host of schemes for extending and supplementing the Vatican Palace and its surroundings. The early fourth century Christian basilica, Christendom's first church, restored and repeatedly redecorated ever more splendidly with paintings and mosaics, stood until the mid-fifteenth century, when Nicholas V, with the support and advice of Alberti, began its reconstruction, which was brought to a halt

*87 Raphael: 'The School of Athens'. Rome: The Vatican. Stanza della Segnatura. Carried out between 1508 and 1511, this series of frescoes is the culmination of Raphael's life's work, and at the same time a complete expression of the classical aims of the Roman High Renaissance in style. An ingenious pictorial programme is developed here, in a composition that is entirely harmonious and at the same time monumental. It introduces the four divisions into which the medieval faculties fell: Theology (*Disputà*—the Disputation of the Sacrament, between the Fathers of the Church); Philosophy ('The School of Athens')—A discussion between Plato and Aristotle concerning questions of ethics and morality in the presence of representatives of the most important Schools of Philosophy in Ancient Greece, and thus a kind of pagan* Sacra Conversazione*; Poetry ('Parnassus'—Apollo guiding the Muses, accompanied by humanity's most sublime poets); and Jurisprudence ('The Bestowal of Canon and Civil Law'). The figures in 'The School of Athens' are recognizable in the main: at the feet of the commanding pair, Plato and Aristotle, are the representatives of the exact sciences (Pythagoras, Euclid and the astronomers). Diogenes, linking philosophy and natural science, reclines on the stairs. The architecture in the background is influenced by Bramante's sketches for the rebuilding of St. Peter's.*

TIMEO
ETIC A.

88 Raphael: 'The School of Athens'. (Detail of Central Section). Rome: The Vatican. Stanza della Segnatura. This detail from the previous illustration shows Plato and Aristotle engaged in disputation. Both these princes of the intellect carry their attributes with them in the form of their chief works: Plato his 'Timaeus', and Aristotle the 'Ethics'. Diogenes the Cynic can be seen (right) at their feet.

Following double page:
89 Raphael: 'Parnassus'. Rome: The Vatican. Stanza della Segnatura. Apollo Musagetes, playing a violin and surrounded by his attendants, the Muses, with their musical instruments and other attributes, is seated in a hilly Olympian landscape not unlike Raphael's Umbrian homeland. Humanity's most illustrious poets, including Blind Homer and Dante (upper left), Sappho (left below), with Petrarch and Boccaccio, appear beside and at the feet of the central group.

however by the Pope's early death. It was not until Julius II, the *terribile,* almost fifty years later that the reconstruction project that stirred Western Christendom was again taken up. In 1506 Bramante was commissioned to work on it. He produced a pure central construction with a cupola, over the ground-plan of a Greek cross, with side-rooms, also dome-vaulted, and apses in the diagonals. His intention was to 'pile the Pantheon on the Temple of Peace (the Constantine or Maxentius Basilica).'

In 1513 Julius II died, followed the year after by Bramante. But the monumental pillars which were to carry the intersection tambour were standing, in spite of everything. Under the new direction, which was taken over by Raphael, Giuliano and Antonio da Sangallo, and Peruzzi, there was a growing tendency to deviate from Bramante's centralized conception in favour of a basilica with nave and two aisles until Michelangelo took over in 1547 and returned to Bramante's original idea, though with some significant alterations. The side halls in the diagonals, which were still basically independent churches or chapels in the Bramante version, were much more strongly integrated into the four arms of the Greek cross, thus apparently shortening them, since it was basically only a question of reinforcing the outer walls and the cupola pillars so as to allow the cupola to dominate the entire space. The cupola was Michelangelo's great concern, and the tambour was completed by the time of his death (1564). Giacomo della Porta enclosed it, and altered the outline laid down by Michelangelo, which was compressed and oppressive, in favour of 'the elegant and optimistic feeling conveyed by the onset of Early Baroque' (H. Keller 1975). (Plates 74 and 75). The central chamber, it is true, fully met the artistic ideals of the High Renaissance, but not the traditional basilica form of the episcopal and monastic churches, nor even the practical requirements of the divine service. Nor was it extensive enough, in spite of its huge size, to receive the influx of believers who wanted to visit the most sacred of churches. Paul V Borghese therefore commissioned Carlo Maderna to place to the east of it a basilica with nave and two aisles.

In 1617 the church was practically completed, but the square in front was still to be decided on. In 1586 Sixtus V had had the 25.50 metre (83′ 8″) high obelisk form Heliopolis—previously in the near-by Circus of Nero—erected by Domenico Fontana in the centre of the square. Maderna created one of the great fountains under commission from Paul V. The second did not arrive as a pendant until the beginning of the eighteenth century. But it needed a genius to co-ordinate and structure the whole vast area and transcendent dimensions of the square. Gianlorenzo Bernini, the outstanding architect and sculptor of Roman High Baroque, solved the problem by again harking back to the style of the late imperial period. He divided the area up into two interlocking squares (1656–1667), one a great transverse oval surrounded by 17 metre (55′ 9″) wide colonnades consisting of four rows of Doric columns and pillars, with a straight architrave whose transverse axis is formed by the obelisks and the Maderna Fountains; and the other a trapezoid square extending and rising up to the façade of the church. The monumental open stairs leading up to the church portals repeat the trapezoid shape of the square. In this way Bernini achieved the perspective effect of making the elongation of the façade seem narrower, while the height increased, allowing it to rise more steeply without seeming to 'fall apart' (Plate 76).

Parallel with the reconstruction of St. Peter's came the extensions and alterations to the Vatican Palace (Plate 77), the equipment and furnishings of which became ever richer and more splendid. (Plates 78 and 79). Around it a number of new structures were assembled, the gem of which, next to the Belvedere and the Stanze and Loggias painted by Raphael (Plates 83–87), was a simple oblong room, the Sistine Chapel (Plate 80). Its fame and glory are the frescoes on walls and ceiling, created by the most famous painters of Umbria and Tuscany, and finally by Michelangelo in the fifteenth and sixteenth centuries. The chapel was built between 1473 and 1484 under Sixtus IV della Rovere and serves ecclesiastical purposes to-day, the most important of

SAPPHO

which is the Conclave, the election of the Pope. It was Sixtus IV also who had the wall-surfaces beneath the windows painted with a cycle of murals by Perugino, Pinturicchio, Botticelli, Ghirlandaio and Signorelli, dealing with Old and New Testament scenes rich in reference to the Pontificate of the commissioning Pope. (Plates 85 and 86). Finally in 1508 Julius II bestowed on Michelangelo the commission to paint the ceiling of the Sistine Chapel. The iconographic theme was the *ante legem* period, that is the period pre-dating the giving of the Laws on Mount Sinai. The nine crossbeams would present the stories of the Creation and the Flood in alternating large and small sections. In the others, seven prophets and five sibyls are enthroned. The four corners of the smaller central panels provide a frame for Nude Youths. 'Michelangelo painted the cycle in reverse chronological order. Instead of beginning on the altar wall with the separation of Light from Darkness, he started out from the entrance wall with the Drunkenness of Noah and painted the First Day of Creation as the last in the series of panels. The colour development inside each of the sections of the ceiling can be understood only if this is borne in mind. When the covers were removed from the first half in 1510 Michelangelo saw his picture from below for the first time. The scale of the figures seemed to him to be too small, and so in the second half he resorted to larger proportions and a smaller number of figures' (H. Keller 1975).

Clement VII de' Medici also commissioned Michelangelo (in 1533) to paint a 'Last Judgement' on the broad wall of the altar (Plate 81), which was 17 metres (55′ 9″) high and 13.30 metres (43′ 7″) broad. Here too Michelangelo was breaking entirely new ground. The twelve Apostles are present, an unusual feature, and the Madonna presses almost anxiously close to the Great Judge, interceding with the Son, who is portrayed nude and without a beard, his head and hair reminiscent of the 'Belvedere Apollo'. The quiet features 'pronounce' no resurrection or damnation. These seem to emanate from the overwhelming soul-saving gesture of the raised arm. 'Any architectonic articulation is avoided in favour of a gigantic rotatory motion: to the left we have the ascent of the Blessed, and to the right the plunging of the Damned.' (H. Keller). Under the influence of the decrees issued by the puritanical Council of Trent and the zealous Pope Paul IV thirty-four nude figures were clothed by Daniele da Volterra.

Even before that, but after the ceiling frescoes, Raphael had designed a series of tapestries, woven in Brussels, which shrouded the most important parts of the chapel.

The assimilating power of the Roman environment is exemplified once more in Raphael. The imprint of the Eternal City, whose prominent artists came almost without exception from outside, made them 'Romans'. In his Umbrian home Perugino's pupil, Raphael, was in no way an outstanding phenomenon. By Roman standards his early work must be adjudged as pale, undistinguished and at times almost boring. In Rome, however, he found his way towards a monumental form: meeting important colleagues, and above all discovering classical antiquity, helped him to become a classic. The ideals of 'classical' painting, closeness to the ancient world, absolute harmony and euphonious, symmetrical composition, and a happy convergence of balanced form and spiritual content, find their most perfect expression in Raphael. With the great frescoes in the Vatican Stanze he attains equality with Michelangelo's work in the Sistine Chapel. In the 'Stanza della Segnatura', created between 1509 and 1511 (Plates 87–90), he developed a complex series of pictures which in concentrated form presents the entire philosophical, religious and aesthetic Renaissance Cosmos. In the centre stands the *Disputà,* a *Sacra Conversazione* in new form, portraying in symbolic disputation all the great exponents of church doctrine on the supreme Christian mystery of the Holy Trinity. In the 'School of Athens' (Plates 87 and 88) Western philosophy makes its appearance in the shape of its most enlightened proponents. Out of this abstract material Raphael has woven a gripping description of actual events. The Ancient World's most important philosophical schools get to grips here with the ultimate questions

90 Raphael: 'The Deliverance of Peter'. Rome: The Vatican. Stanza d'Eliodoro. The frescoes in this room were created from 1512 to 1514 as additions to the 'Stanza della Segnatura'. Raphael here underwent an astonishing change, from the classical, calm moderation of the 'Disputà' and 'The School of Athens' to a much more expressive and active 'baroque' style, all within the space of a few years. This is particularly clear in the 'Deliverance of Peter', where the centre of interest lies in the portrayal of light manifest almost in baroque fashion. The colouring has undergone a fundamental change in order to achieve this effect.

90

affecting humanity. In the centre we recognize Plato and Aristotle, the most outstanding of the wise men. The reference made here to the Christian *Disputa* is of course deliberate. A resonant pillared hall provides the solemn background, which is reminiscent of Bramante's plans for the reconstruction of St. Peter's, which date from the same period.

91 Raphael: 'The Triumph of Galatea' (Detail). Rome: Villa Farnesina. This fresco, painted by Raphael's own hand in 1514, belongs to a series of mythological and astrological frescoes carried out at the beginning of the sixteenth century for the Roman villa of the banker, art-patron and humanist Agostino Chigi by artists such as Giulio Romano, Francesco Penni, and Giovanni da Udine. After the earnest and weighty sequence of paintings in the Vatican, Raphael and his colleagues here introduce the other side of the High Renaissance, which is full of the ancient world's mythology and erotic splendour. In the Sala di Galatea (originally a ground-level loggia leading to the open garden area) a complex set of horoscopic and astrological illustrations appears on the ceiling (Baldasarre Peruzzi), together with Ovid's Metamorphoses (the lunettes) and 'The Triumph of Galatea'. Galatea glides over the sea in a scallop-shell chariot drawn by a team of dolphins, surrounded by her retinue of playful Nereids and Naiads. Her brilliant red robe, effectively contrasting with the lovely luminous figure, flutters like 'love's banner' swelling in the wind. Raphael came even closer in this tableau than in the Vatican Stanze *to his goal and ideal, the fresco of classical antiquity, a few examples of which had just been discovered by archaeologists.*

Page following:
92 Raphael: 'Venus, Ceres and Juno'. Rome, Villa Farnesina. Garden loggia. Working under Raphael's guidance and in keeping with the free and cheerful schemes designed for the Renaissance villa, Giulio Romano and Francesco Penni painted this summerhouse with scenes from the classical myth of Cupid and Psyche, as told by Apuleius in his Golden Ass. *Raphael kept the figures on the spandrel (our illustration) for himself. Working in a classical spirit similar to that of the ancient Greeks and Romans, he came nearer to the physical ideal of classical antiquity in these vigorous and lively gods and goddesses than any other painter of the Roman High Renaissance. The ornamental motifs—festoons of fruit and foliage friezes—are by Giovanni da Udine. The curved surface above the windows (below right in our illustration) is decorated with classicizing 'grotesques'. The first authentic classical frescoes had just been discovered in Nero's Golden House at this date and this type of decoration was known as 'grotesque'* (grotteschi) *because Nero's staterooms, now covered with rubble, lay deep underground and so conveyed the impression of being subterranean grottoes.*

In the 'Parnassus' (Plate 89) Poetry is represented as the third medieval 'Faculty'. In the centre is Apollo, with his lyre transformed into a *viola da braccio*. He is surrounded by the Muses with their attributes, and accompanied by the most outstanding poets. In the left-hand upper section we recognize Blind Homer and next to him Dante's characteristic profile. Left below, with a scroll, is Sappho. An idealized Olympian hill landscape reminiscent of Raphael's Umbrian home acts as a backcloth. In another Stanza Raphael painted 'The Deliverance of Peter' from prison, by the Angel (Plate 90), in effect an extraordinarily modern representation of a 'vision of illumination', which is more effective still when we remember that the mural is sited on a wall between two windows so that natural daylight shares in the pictorial impression produced.

Raphael leads us into a purely classical world with the mythological cycle in the Villa Farnesina (Plates 91 and 92). Here he reveals the entire spectrum of the ancient world of mythology and the Hellenic love-story of Cupid and Psyche, in pictures full of grace, erotic humour and classical serenity. Contemporaries considered that these images were unsurpassable. Any 'post' or 'after' style was inconceivable. Raphael's importance in the intervening period is no longer so highly estimated, due perhaps to the adulation accorded him from the sixteenth to the eighteenth century and the ensuing nineteenth-century exaggeration. By Goethe's time he was considered to be *the* classic par excellence, and his achievement equated with Dante's *Divine Comedy*. To-day he appears to many art-lovers to be academic, dry, merely sweet and complaisant, or even cold and polished to perfection. This reversal of judgement is no doubt as unjust as his uncritical apotheosis a hundred years ago. The selection of paintings shown here for comparison may demonstrate that his genius has no reason to fear: it easily measures up to that of Michelangelo or Titian.

A second great building project of Julius II within the walls of the Vatican was the Villa Belvedere. The actual Villa, begun under Innocent VIII and destined to house the earliest and most important collection of antiquities ('Laocoön' and the 'Apollo Belvedere') following Bramante's architectural alterations to the inner courtyard, must be accorded the minimum of space in this text. The determining factor is the layout of the garden, surrounded as it is by façade walls on three levels complete with windows and pilasters, and stretching originally over three terraces from the upper Belvedere to the lower exedra. Open stairways communicate between the various terraces, the revetment walls of which, in the central axis, were here and there provided with niche grottoes and water displays. The lower garden could be flooded to arrange 'Sea-Battles' and water-ballets. In extent and conception the gardens are comparable only to the Praeneste sanctuary, which consciously influenced Bramante and Pirro Ligorio, who created the crowning exedra; or with the great imperial villas (the Hadrian, say, in Tivoli) which is why this miracle of open-space architecture is always referred to as the 'classical villa'.

'Rome is Bernini,' said Rodin, and in fact Gianlorenzo Bernini, architect and sculptor, symbolizes the last great age of Roman art, the Baroque. Together with his much more headstrong and unorthodox but no less highly-gifted opposite, Borromini, he once more enriched the seventeenth-century landscape of Rome with palaces, churches and squares representing the last and perhaps the greatest pinnacle of Roman art. Baroque signifies the 'total work of art' to which architecture, sculpture and painting, but also the decorative arts, municipal architecture and horticultural art, are subordinated. The façades of squares correspond to the concave and convex church façades, while bold vaulting constructions made it possible for painters like Andrea Pozzo or Pietro da Cortona to produce in palaces and churches gigantic ceiling paintings, brilliant in their perspective effects. Their superabundance of baroque allegories glorified the owners, or raised, with the most ecstatic religious feeling, Heavenly Father, Son, Madonna and all the saints into celestial glory. All of them, artists, Popes and saints seemed in the seventeenth century to be conscious of one duty only: to bring to completion the beauty and greatness of Rome.

Venice

Venice was a paradox
(M. Langewiesche)

A city of world rank that was never fortified.

A conglomeration of houses, palaces and churches, erected on that most insubstantial and undependable of foundations, the sea.

A state, of world rank, whose stability and political significance was based in the last analysis on nothing more than the rolling ship's timbers of its merchant fleet, but which nevertheless endured for longer than any organized state of to-day.

An organized state surrounded by enemies in its immediate vicinity, for example those who commanded the rivers flowing into the Venetian lagoon, the Po, Adige and Brenta. No maritime republic—not Pisa, Genoa or Amalfi—could have been so easily surrounded and starved into submission as Venice. That this did not happen is a tribute to Venetian statesmanship.

Venice became great not because of but in spite of its situation. It is not surprising therefore that twentieth-century Ventice still looks back on its past with pride and an awareness of tradition.

Any observant traveller who pays several visits to Venice, using the various forms of transport available to-day, comes up against this paradox even before his arrival in the lagoon city. Driving by car from Padua he reads, with

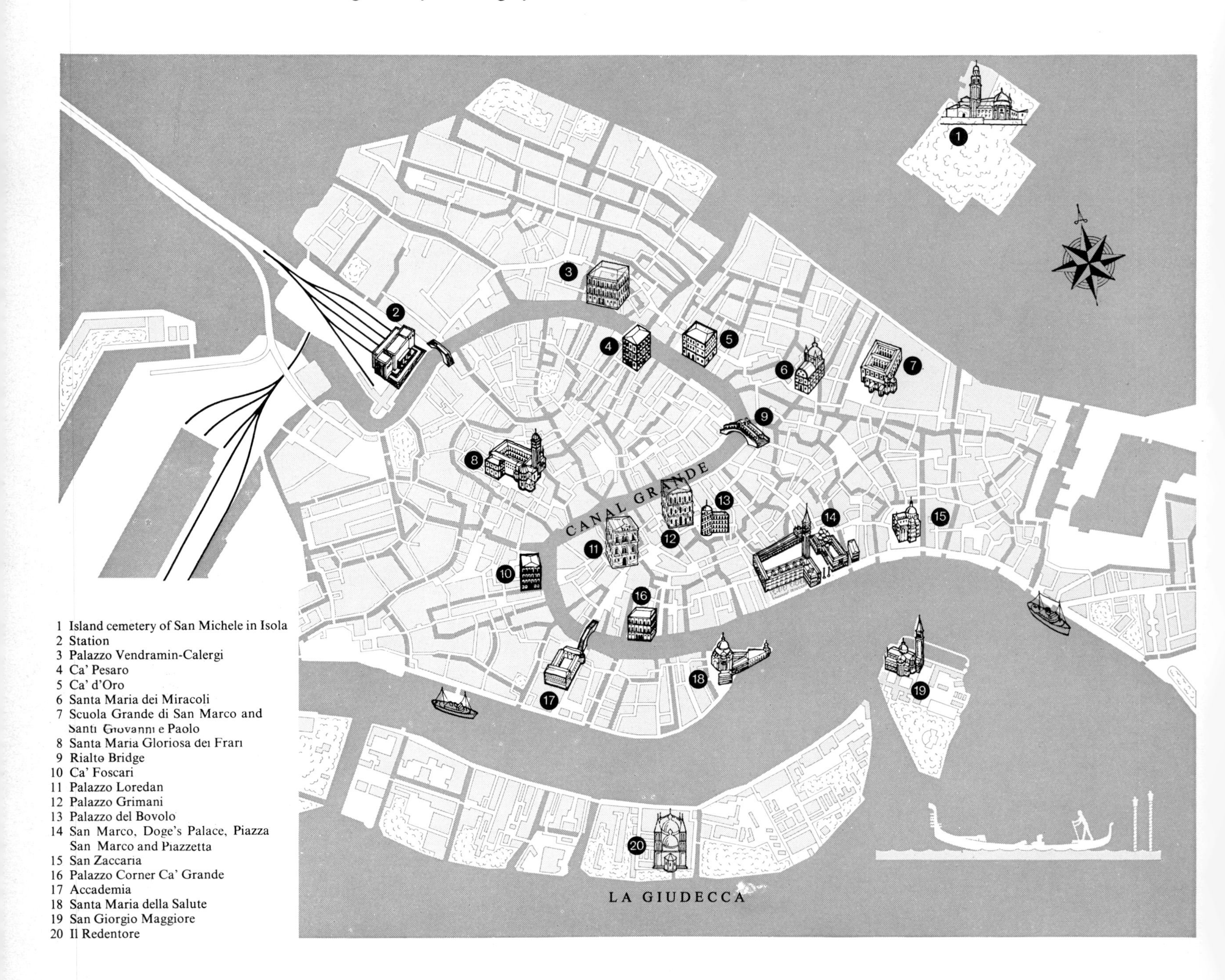

some astonishment, at the entrance to the motorway some forty kilometres (twenty-four miles) out: 'Autostrada della Serenissima'.

Above it he is greeted by the Lion of St. Mark in relief, the relevant gospel open between his paws at the words: 'Pax tibi, Marce, evangelista meus' ('Peace be unto thee, Mark, my apostle'). The same Lion sits enthroned on vertical pylons along the railway lines leading across the lagoon-embankment into the city. You can even recognize the symbol at the airport, in the middle of the industrial zone of Mestre. Arriving by sea—still the most splendid way of reaching the city—the traveller as he passes by can see the Lion on a high column above the Piazzetta (Plate 98). What is the significance of the 'Serenissima' (Serene Highness) and the Lion that still greet and welcome everyone to-day with such pride and awareness of tradition, almost two hundred years after the Venetian Republic's downfall? The Lion is the symbol of the patron-saint of an international empire, and a city-state scattered over a hundred and twenty islands in the midst of the North Adriatic lagoons. Its houses, palaces and churches were built on piles, hundreds of thousands of oak, alder and larch props. This State, apparently so vulnerable, stood longer than any other realm in our later history, be it democracy, oligarchy or government by king or emperor. Neither Greece, the 'cradle of the West', nor the Roman Empire, nor the Holy Roman Empire that encompassed and united nations, lasted as long. Venice alone can boast that in all its near one thousand years of existence no enemy conqueror ever set foot on its soil.

However select, noble and rich Venetian art appears in architecture and the fine arts, especially painting, the greatest work of art created here is the Venetian state itself. Only those who know Venice's history are able to understand and properly appreciate the art of the city.

History

The Venetians dwelt, far from the internal and external strife that was shaking the Roman Empire, on the shores and lagoons of the Northern loop of the Adriatic. Agriculture, but mainly fishing and salt-mining, gave them sustenance. The storms of the great migrations, the invasions of Visigoths, Ostrogoths, Langobards, and Huns, who destroyed Aquileia, seat of the Patriarch, in 453, drove the population further and further out into the lagoon. Only those to whom that element was native could know the treacherous nature of the shoals and the sandbanks lying under water and could make use of them for their own defence.

At the end of the seventh century, in 697, these tiny and often mutually hostile 'city-states', such as Grado, where the Patriarch of Aquileia had fled, Caorle, Eraclea, Jesolo, Torcello, Chioggia and Malamocco, united and elected a common head, the Doge. They crowned him with the sailor's cap pinched out in front, the *cornu ducale,* placed themselves under the protection of the Exarchate of Ravenna, thereby coming within the Byzantine Province in Italy.

In 809 Pepin, son of Charlemagne, took Friuli and Istria and pushed forward into the Venetian settlements in the lagoon. Chioggia and Malamocco, until then the largest settlement, were destroyed. The 10th Doge, Angelo Partecipazio, thereafter transferred the seat of government, in 811, to the largest of the islands in the most central lagoon, the 'Rivo alto', the modern Rialto. Thus Venice was founded.

Fishermen and peasants had fled to the lagoon, but with them also were well-to-do merchants from *terra firma,* who had become wealthy through the salt-trade, in Padua and Verona. Their names, Orseola, Morosini, Loredan and Pisani, the oldest aristocratic names in Europe, were to appear more than once in future on the list of Doges. These young merchant families showed the new state the only path it could take, namely trade, on their familiar element, the sea. The perils inherent in Venice's geographical and political position were also to be its opportunity.

Double page following:
93 Venice: Piazzetta with the West façade of St. Mark's and the West Wing of the Doge's Palace. The splendid façade of St. Mark's, with its coloured mosaics set in white marble filigree, links up here with the west side of the Doge's Palace almost without leaving a trace, thereby giving very clear expression to the identity of Church and State. On the right, situated in front of the Campanile, we see the Loggetta, a choice piece of architecture by Jacopo Sansovino, dating from 1537 to 1540. Behind it is the façade of the Library. The changing play of light and shadow seems to give the Piazzetta's architectural lines new and different structures at various times.

QVIS FRACTIS PORTIS SPOLIAT ME CAMPIO FORTIS
EN VERVS FORTIS QVI FREGIT VINCVLA MORTIS

Torn between the declining but still powerful empire in the East, Byzantium, and the growing Holy Roman Empire which was able to reward its vassals and margraves, not only north of the Alps but also in northern Italy, with rich presents and domains for their loyalty and dependability, Venice developed a diplomacy which over the years became more and more subtle: *bilancia,* playing the great powers off against one another, and keeping a wary eye on new expanding forces, whether the Papal state or the competing maritime republics, Genoa, Amalfi and Pisa, the powerful city-states in Upper Italy or, later, the Hapsburgs. Venice's ambassadors were the best-informed in Europe, and reported everything back to Venice with a fidelity that was rare. Modern historians still use this inexhaustible source of information.

The merchants who brought the young state to full flower were practical, deliberate and to the point in thought and action. Yet along with their city they were bound up with the early Middle Ages. They were well aware therefore that a city, and even more a state with ambitions to rule the Mediterranean, needed a powerful and significant patron saint, and, being merchants, they knew how much quality counted. Very little was known about San Teodoro, Venice's first saint, an early Christian martyr. The fact that the first church consecrated to him was in Byzantium meant little in their eyes. But a monastery in Alexandria harboured the remains of one of the four apostles, St. Mark. The Doge, Justinian Partecipazio, dispatched a delegation to the monastery concerned in 828. The Venetians had had the best of trading relations with the Arab rulers of the territory for some considerable time. After some semblance of threat to the monastery on the part of Arabs bribed by the Venetians, the Republic's emissaries managed to acquire the saint's body for fifty *zecchini.* Concealed under a layer of pork, which to the Mohammedans was unclean, the saint reached Venice safe and sound. He is said to have performed numerous miracles during his trip over, and these were later recorded by Tintoretto in a splendid cycle which was a culminating point in Venetian painting. The saint's remains were at first lodged in the palace of the Duke, now the Doge's Palace, until the present church of St. Mark was built in his honour in the eleventh century. That meant that the priceless relic rested in the Doge's Palace church, which was what St. Mark's was, until the year 1807. The State had its patron saint, and the banner with the Lion, the saint's symbolic animal, was to wave in future from Brescia, fronting the gates of Milan, to Constantinople; from the battlements of Split and Candia in Crete; from Corfu and Famagusta in Cyprus; and from Chios and Ravenna. From now on 'Viva San Marco!' meant 'Viva Venezia!'.

Venice was still Byzantium's ally, even if only nominally, and under its protection. Trade relations were close, but the ageing city on the Hellespont had to pay for every atom of support accorded it in the expanding Republic by new concessions, wrung out of it. It was Venetian money and diplomacy that promoted relations between Byzantium and the Emperor; and Venetian ships and weapons that protected the Byzantine colonies in the Adriatic against the rapacious Saracens. When Venice, together with Byzantium, drove the Normans out of the Adriatic and Eastern Mediterranean at the end of the eleventh century, Venice's demands seemed quite modest: no territory or money, simply a trade and staple monopoly. In actual fact Byzantium was too weak to defend its Adriatic colonies, especially along the Dalmatian coast. The Dalmatian states therefore turned to Venice for help against pirates and Serbs and Croats from the hinterland. In about 1000, when the Christian West was paralysed by a vision of the imminent end of the world, the Doge, Pietro Orseolo II, began soberly and systematically to take over the Eastern Adriatic coast, a process in which Zara or Rugusa and the other towns were not exactly 'subjugated' but made the subject of alliances with one aim in mind: free trade for the lagoon city and secure bases for the Venetian fleet. The towns willingly accepted the terms imposed because Venice guaranteed their security. And as Venice in the fifteenth century united with the cities on *terra firma* so it proceeded now: *Pro summa*

94 Venice: San Marco. Lunette on the second Northern side-entrance of the West façade. The semi-circular mosaic was created in Rococo style and carried out by Leopoldo dal Pozzo in 1728 from a sketch by Sebastiano Ricci, G. B. Tiepolo's contemporary and teacher. In a design that is still almost Titianesque it portrays the veneration accorded to the body of St. Mark by the Venetian authorities.

95 Venice: Piazza San Marco. Unlike the Piazzetta the Piazza has to manage without the sea acting as a fourth boundary wall. Its contours are therefore harder, and light and shadow more clearly defined. The even rows of arcades of the Old Procurator's office, and the geometric pattern of the square, almost convey the impression of some 'interior'.

fide summus amor, 'for the greatest faith the greatest love.'

Venice's successes in foreign policy were paralleled by the evolution internally of a stable political system, in which order was guaranteed by irrevocable laws. Yet there was some apprehension perhaps that in the future not every Doge would exhibit selfless devotion to the Republic. So in 1172 the Grand Council, the Maggior Consiglio, came into being. This was the political creation of a constitution which had already been put into practice, and from now on would endure for another six hundred years and even then be abrogated only under pressure from outside. The sober rationale behind the constitution was not confined within the limits of any inflexible ideology. It was as objectively conceived as the democracy of early Roman times: as élitist as the Greek oligarchy; and where affairs of state, i.e. Venice's existence, so required, almost over-cautious in the checks and balances of office.

At the top stood the Doge, elected for life by the Maggior Consiglio. Though the city had 120 of these in all, no more than half-a-dozen bearers of the recurrent aristocratic names emerged from obscurity to enter history as distinct personalities.

In their case the element of extreme good fortune or of great momentary peril was always present, as with Enrico Dandolo (1192–1205), who conquered Byzantium for Venice, or Marino Falier (1354–55), who wanted to change the constitution, and was beheaded on the steps of the Doge's Palace, his head and trunk left lying for days in the Cortile, as a warning. Francesco Foscari (1423–1457), a *condottiere*-type, and a Renaissance man of violence, decided on conquest of the *terra firma*, and had as a result to leave the Eastern Mediterranean to the Turks. Whether his decision was right or wrong, the wheel of history can never be put into reverse. In any case he was deposed because of his autocratic rule and his son sent into exile. Finally, Francesco Morosini (1688–1694), a born commander-in-chief, should be mentioned; he was able for a brief period to regain the Venetian colonies in the Levant and on the Peloponnese from the Turks. To some extent the Maggior Consiglio was the Republic's 'Parliament'. It could meet without the Doge. Originally every male 'citizen' over twenty-five years of age was a member if his family had been settled in Venice for several generations. Next to the Maggior Consiglio stood the Senate, the Upper House, so to speak, of the Venetian Parliament and its legislative bodies. The Doge and members of the Collegio met here with some two hundred elected Senators. The Collegio was the Government Cabinet and consisted of some twenty-five members elected from the Maggior Consiglio.

In the fourteenth century the notorious 'Consiglio dei Dieci', the notorious 'Council of Ten', was formed from members of the Collegio. This was an emergency measure to speed up parliamentary procedure when urgent decisions had to be taken. Practically all important matters, or those which were out of the ordinary, were discussed in secret session here. Two members of the Council of Ten were appointed State Inquisitors, with one function only, to investigate, together with a Council of the Doge's, the one crime that Venice punished unmercifully, high treason.

Independent only in appearance, therefore, it was possible for each institution to be represented in the others through committees elected from within, so that each institution controlled the other.

Any political system with a constitution based on cool and sober calculation which also excludes from government both people and citizens must try to find ways of making its abstractions not only clear to all but pleasing. Religious commitment, mystical transformation and solemn ritual were there to hand.

'Viva San Marco!' stood for 'Viva Venezia!' Not surprisingly, therefore, the Procurators of St. Mark's, the 'canons' of the state church and guardians of the patron-saint occupied a particularly high position in the state apparatus. Next to the Doge they were the highest dignitaries in the Serenissima. They alone wore purple and walked in the great processions immediately behind the Doge. And once a year the Doge, too, emerged from the anonymity of his magnificent prison to join in the glamour of public festival, surrounded by all the radiant pomp of the Serenissima. Once a year, on Ascension Day, the *Sensa,* the Doge sailed out to sea aboard the ship of state, the gilded Bucintoro, accompanied by hundreds of craft, including gondolas. No dignitary of state dared absent himself. There the Doge wed the waters again, casting his ring into the sea with the words: *Desponsamus te mare; in signo veri perpetuique domini* ('We marry thee, sea, in the sign of the one True and Eternal Lord').

In 1177 Venetian statesmanship and diplomacy triumphed for the first time over the two strongest powers of the period, Pope and Emperor. Possessed by the desire to take over northern Italy, Frederick I Barbarossa nominated three anti-popes, since the legitimate Pope, Alexander III, opposed his plans. The Emperor destroyed Milan and the Pope fled to France. Not until Alexander had placed himself at the head of the League of Lombard Towns and the Emperor had been defeated at the Battle of Legnano in 1176 did any hope exist that the two bitter enemies could be persuaded to make peace. Venice acted as mediator and arranged (or even 'forced') a meeting in Venice between Emperor and Pope, thus bringing about a reconciliation. It was Venice's first international success. For its services, from both parties of course, it demanded only customs and tax concessions.

96

In 1204 the ninety-six-year-old and almost blind Doge Enrico Dandolo led against Byzantium the army of Crusaders, which had assembled some 35–40,000 men in Venice for the Fourth Crusade. The Crusaders had come to the city in the hope that the Republic would place its fleet at their disposal to liberate the Holy Sepulchre from the Turks. After exhausting, long-drawn-out negotiations, Venice presented two conditions. Zara (Zadar) on the Adriatic coast must be won back and—here came the stunner—first of all Christian Byzantium, regarded as impregnable, must be taken. Dynastic quarrels in Byzantium provided the threadbare excuse. Basically, as was always the case when Venice had a hand in the game, it was a question of commercial profit. Byzantium held the staple monopoly for every commodity traded in the East. It was therefore able to stockpile these until they fetched the highest prices, a type of competition that had to be eliminated. And not only that. The last hour had struck for the old East Roman capital. The Crusaders did in fact burn and plunder Byzantium, but the major share of the booty passed to Venice. The ancient bronze horses, the four in hand, which ever since, apart from a brief sojourn in Napoleon's Paris, have stood above the main portal of St. Mark's (Plate 93), as well as hundreds of columns, capitals and the finest marble statuary, whether complete or in pieces—all these were brought to St. Mark's so that the southern side of the church

96 and 97 Venice: Piazza San Marco: Torre dell' Orologio (Clock Tower) erected in the years 1496–1499 by Mauro Coducci. Multicoloured marble incrustations, elegantly executed in detail, shape the structure of the three-storeyed tower, on the roof of which bronze figures, called 'Mori' (Moors), strike the hours with their hammers. The first floor contains the sundial, with the signs of the Zodiac (Plate 97) and gold and enamel inlays, while the second has a statue of the Madonna, with two panels at the sides showing the hours and minutes respectively. On the third floor is the Lion of St. Mark against a blue celestial background decorated with golden stars. The arched gateway leads through to the merceria, *market lanes stretching as far as the Rialto, which to-day remains the chief shopping-centre for Venetians and foreigners alike.*

97

became a triumphant wall of captured trophies. Innumerable reliquaries with their precious shrines enriched the Saint's Treasury. Feeling that his task had been completed, Enrico Dandolo died in Byzantium and was buried in the gallery of the Hagia Sophia.

At that time, in 1204, the Maggior Consiglio was even considering the outrageous possibility of moving to Byzantium, which would probably have decisively altered the history of Europe. The plan was rejected by two votes.

Quite apart from its plans for conquest, Venice had greatly profited from providing the Crusaders with transport, though it did incur in the process serious competition from Pisa and Genoa. By the middle of the fourteenth century, indeed, Genoa was strong enough to represent a mortal threat to Venice, unless the Serenissima managed to beat back the rival maritime republic, i.e. drive its ships out of the Adriatic at least. For a long time Genoa

99

had ruled the Western Mediterranean, but its vessels, under the leadership of the shrewd and courageous family of the Doria, were now penetrating into the Adriatic. They made allies of Venice's enemies, the Emperor, the King of Hungary, the Archduke of Tyrol, and even with Venice's greatest and nearest neighbour on *terra firma,* Padua, and its princely family, the Carrara. Venetian galleys, true enough, did patrol the Adriatic day and night from 1378 to 1379 to halt the advance of the Genoese fleet, but without result, despite the most strenuous effort and sacrifice. Genoa and its allies took Trieste, Grado fell, and finally, with the aid of the Carrara, Chioggia. Summoning up every ounce of their strength and material resources, the Venetians feverishly built a new fleet which in the end, if it did not succeed in winning Chioggia back, at least blockaded it for six months. In June 1380, Genoa surrendered. Venice had suffered grievous losses, but the Genoese advance had been stopped.

In 1423 Doge Tomaso Mocenigo, on his deathbed, laid before the Serenissima the following statistics: Venice had 190,000 inhabitants. Out of a trade balance of 10 million ducats, 4 million went to Venice in profits. 3000 smaller vessels sailed the seas under the Lion Banner, their crews consisting of 17,000 seamen. There were 300 large merchantmen with 8,000 sailors, and 45 galleys with 11,000, plus 16,000 ship's carpenters. Including sailmakers, ropemakers, saddlers, coopers, dockers, plus harbour and customs officials,

Previous double page:
98 Venice: The Doge's Palace. A full view of the Doge's Palace reveals how conscious of tradition people were, in the matter of architecture, for almost two centuries and how much they clung, despite much destruction, to concepts they had accepted: light and airy open ground-floors, and an apparently compact but nevertheless looser structured upper storey, with its textile-like wall pattern. The battlements obviously served no defensive purpose but were a crowning decoration only. In front stood the lagoon-city's symbols: two monumental granite columns, also imported from the East, with Byzantine capitals. One bore the statue of St. Theodore, Venice's first patron saint, and the other the original bronze figure of the Lion of St. Mark, once a chimera of Assyrian, Persian or Sassanid derivation. At the foot of the columns figural groups can still be seen, probably twelfth-century, which represent fishmongers and greengrocers, with coopers and others, indicating that the market was held on this side of the Piazzetta before the Library was erected.

99 *Venice: The Doge's Palace. The Bridge of Sighs (Ponte dei Sospiri). A canal separates the rear of the Doge's Palace from a wing added by Pietro Lombardo in Early Renaissance style after the fire in 1483. Since about 1600 there has been a covered connecting bridge, leading from the Doge's Palace to the cells, for those guilty of offences against the State. Despite the name, it is an elegant and attractive structure.*

almost half of the citizens and inhabitants of Venice were engaged in shipping. The Republic's arsenal was the largest dockyard of the period in the world, and could fit out twenty-five galleys in fourteen days.

Venice's houses were valued at seven million ducats, from which the city drew rents amounting to half a million. A thousand nobles, including most of the merchants, had incomes of between seventy and four thousand ducats per annum, but the size of personal income exercised no influence over individual or family ratings.

The national income that year was 1,100,000 ducats, higher therefore than that of France, England, Spain, Milan, Florence or the Curia, though by 1450 it had slipped back to 800,000. If we remember that, in addition, Venice had introduced a number of small or rather specialized industries into its territory, and gave them every encouragement, it is easy to see that the citizens' standard of living was more than satisfactory.

The glass industry at Murano enjoyed special benefits. Venice's glass factories had been moved to the island in 1291 on account of the danger of fire. Murano's population enjoyed particular advantages due to their artistic skill. They had their own *libro d'oro,* a Golden Book in which the names of their distinguished citizens were entered, just as in Venice's Great Golden Book, but the secret of the art of glass-blowing was strictly guarded. A glass-blower who left the Republic was in his absence sentenced to death. Conversely, in 1524, a glass-blower who had fled because of a murder was pardoned on his return.

Tolerance of anything which did not harm the Serene Republic was always Venice's unfailing motto. The position of the Jews up to the seventeenth century was better than in any other state. There had never been any pogroms. In 1132 over thirteen hundred Jews were living in the city. They could carry on their trade without any restriction, and even practise as doctors. Until 1374 they lived on the Giudecca (hence the name of that largest of the islands, directly opposite the city), or in Mestre. They received permission to settle in Venice itself on payment of a tax. Moneylending and usury helped them to control the trade in gold, silver and jewellery, until 1395. They were not, however, allowed to own any property, and had to wear distinctive clothing. They were also forbidden to marry Christians, or have anything to do with Christian women, even courtesans. From 1516 on they lived in the *ghetto.* This was a quarter which had originally housed foundries. In Italian the word *gettare* means, *inter alia,* to smelt metal, or cast iron.

Venice proved to be just as tolerant in times of religious fanaticism. No ecclesiastical inquisition, no witch-hunts or burning of heretics disturbed the calm, industrious life of the city. Giordano Bruno found refuge there after a restless life of wandering, until the Papal Inquisition carried him off to Rome and burned him as a heretic in 1600. Many Protestants fled to Venice after the wars of religion, from Catholic countries which forbade them to practise their religion. Books placed on the Index outside Venice were printed and published in the city, so that, as might have been expected, many of the Republic's publishers, printers, makers of woodcuts and copper-plate engravers opened up new branches.

In the late Middle Ages, when awakening self-awareness among the middle classes and manual workers led in the larger towns of the Empire and the city-republics to political aspirations, and social protest against compulsory guild 'unionization', Venice remained calm. People were comparatively prosperous. They had work, and even though the prosperous middle class, especially the merchants, remained barred from government affairs after the 'Serrata' of 1297, there was ample opportunity to acquire prominence among one's fellow-citizens as a well-to-do patron, to celebrate festivals, hold conferences, in other words establish one's position in the community.

There was in particular the institution of the *Scuole,* as they had called themselves since the thirteenth century (and before that probably either *ars* or *confraternità).* They were unique in the social and cultural history of Europe, and could be associations of manual workers for example, rather like the

100

guilds, or even ethnic groups, such as the Slavs, Greeks or Albanians living in Venice. These *Scuole* had their own chapels and hospitals which took in guests, and also the sick, as well as club-rooms. They 'combined the benevolent aims of the freemasons with the devotional exercises of religious brotherhoods'. (H. Honour, 1966). They would visit prisoners in custody and paid for the burial services of those excuted. Members undertook religious duties, and assisted their colleagues in time of need or sickness. Their organizations were financed out of members' annual dues, which normally yielded a not inconsiderable surplus, which was used to improve the club-rooms. Every great painter in Venice, from Cima da Conegliano, the Bellinis, father and son, to Tintoretto and Tiepolo were given important commissions to paint chapels and club-rooms. Only Titian, prince of painters, had no time for such pursuits. Tintoretto, for instance, known for the passion with which he painted, as if possessed, took twenty-four years (1564–1588) to finish the thirty gigantic frescoes on the ceiling and walls of the Scuola di San Rocco.

At the start of the fifteenth century, soon after Doge Mocenigo had

100 Venice: The Doge's Palace: Inner Courtyard and Scala dei Giganti. Specifically Venetian-Byzantine forms were adhered to in the external structure of the Doge's Palace, even after numerous fires. The Eastern façade on the other hand, under Antonio Rizzo (1483 to 1498) and later Pietro Lombardo, took on the rich decorative forms of the Early Venetian Renaissance. In front rises the monumental Scala dei Giganti (Giants' Staircase), erected from a design by Rizzo, and dating between 1484 and 1501. It is dominated by two over-life-size figures of Neptune and Mars, created by Jacopo Sansovino in 1554, and symbolizing the fact that Venice's mastery of the seas must be upheld, by war if need be. The Doge was crowned in the podium at the top of the staircase.

101 Venice: The Doge's Palace: Golden Staircase (Scala d'Oro). This small and rather narrow stairway is the continuation of the Scala dei Giganti inside and is famous for the costly gilt stucco décor. The Doge Andrea Gritti commissioned the decoration in 1538. Sansovino and Alessandro Vittoria are named as the artists responsible for its design and execution. The stairs were solely for the use of leading citizens of the Serenissima and prominent State guests.

Double page following:
102 Venice: The Doge's Palace: Sala del Anticollegio (Collegial Entrance Hall). This was designed as a waiting-room for selected visitors being admitted to the Doge's presence. It was restored after the fire of 1574 or 1577, from designs by Palladio and Scamozzi, with richly gilt plasterwork and ceiling frescoes. The most important items are Tintoretto's and Veronese's murals, including Tintoretto's 'Minerva', who—protecting Venice and Peace—is repulsing Mars; and Veronese's 'Rape of Europa', a picture typically Venetian in that Europa does not look as though she has been raped but is cheerfully mounting the gaily-decorated bull kneeling humbly before her.

Pages 168–169
103 Venice: The Doge's Palace: Sala dello Scrutinio. (Election Chamber). The Scrutini, *who belonged to the Maggior Consiglio, elected the Doge in the last resort. Decorated previously in costly fashion by Tintoretto and Pordenone, the work was again undertaken by the School of Tintoretto and Veronese after the 1577 fire. Clearly recognizable is the Venetian principle in ceiling decoration of placing the canvasses in richly carved gilt frames, which could be up to a metre (3' 3'') in depth. On the narrow side of the room stands the Arch erected in 1694, on the ancient Roman model, to honour Francesco Morosini, who was able for a brief period to win back for Venice the Peloponnese, and hence the Eastern Mediterranean.*

101

presented his proud balance-sheet to the city bearing evidence of much prosperity, Venice experienced its first serious crisis. The face of the world was changing. The Mediterranean, which Venice ruled, became rather an unimportant inland sea as far as maritime commerce was concerned. On May 29, 1453, Mohammed II captured Constantinople. The very next day he entered the Hagia Sophia and while the Moslem priest was preaching the creed of Islam from the pulpit, the conqueror sent up a prayer to Allah, his face turned towards Mecca, and had Enrico Dandolo's ashes scattered to the four winds. Venice was obliged to give up the major part of the Cyclades and her colonies on Euboea. In 1492 Columbus, seeking a western passage to India, discovered the American continent. Between 1497 and 1498 Vasco da Gama became the first to round the Cape of Good Hope, thus discovering the sea-route to the East Indies. All the commercial goods from Asia which had reached the Eastern shores of the Mediterranean via the land routes, there to be loaded on to Venetian galleys, were unloaded in Spanish and Portuguese ports, cleared through customs, and marketed. Not long afterwards the Maggior Consiglio was again discussing the project of venturing a break-out from the Mediterranean into the Red Sea, anticipating the later Suez Canal. But Venice was too exhausted to undertake any such bold and epoch-making venture.

With its centuries of experience and gift of foreseeing periods of political change, Venice had understood in advance of all these events that the Republic would have to take new and opposing paths if it were to survive.

FRANCISCO
MAVROCENO
PELOPONNESIACO
SENATVS
ANNO MDCVIC

Open so far only seaward, especially towards the East, and interceding in land disputes only when it saw its maritime commerce threatened, the city now turned to the mainland. There farming opportunities offered themselves, in which unemployed seamen and ships' carpenters could find work. There too, now as before, lay the important trade routes to the North, which had to be grasped. Treviso, Conegliano and Castelfranco had been taken as early as 1339, to secure these same trade-routes. In 1405 Padua and Verona fell after bitter struggles with the Garrara and della Scala, as Vicenza had fallen in the previous year, while Udine and the whole of Friuli became part of the Republic in 1454. The standard of St. Mark had even flown from Ravenna's market-square, between 1430 and 1454, before the city, to its misfortune, was retaken by the Papal States. Brescia fell in 1441. Venice now found itself before the gates of Milan, which was to become its most bitter adversary. The fifteenth century thus saw Venice embark on the occupation of the mainland. Here too, however mercilessly they had once expelled, tortured and killed the ruling princes, the Venetians set up a good, peaceful and just system of government in the cities, and though columns bearing the Lion of St. Mark might be erected in the market-squares, or Venice's clock-tower and Campanile imitated in Udine or Verona, the Lion still proclaimed *Pax tibi, Marce, Evangelista meus,* and for the vassal cities the maxim held as of old: *Pro summa fide summus amor.*

The aristocracy and prosperous bourgeoisie, in the captive cities and in Venice alike, grasped the changed economic situation astonishingly quickly. The merchants became feudal barons and landed proprietors. They went to *villegiature* (summer holiday resorts), especially since poets and philosophers had been glorifying their vision of 'country-life' since the start of the Renaissance. They had their villas built by Palladio, Sanmicheli, Sansovino and other important architects of the period, but directly in front of the stately columned porticos, vineyards, orchards and tilled fields stretched away into the distance, differing entirely from the villas of Roman and Florentine patricians, where large, artistically planned Renaissance gardens comprised all the surroundings.

The quarrel with Milan lasted for decades. Both city-states were in the end exhausted, and in 1514 a mutual guarantee treaty was signed, which included the other great power on Italian soil apart from the Papal state—Florence. Meantime, however, France entered the lists, having recovered from the wounds inflicted by the Hundred Years' War with England and now unified internally. Charles VIII marched through the entire peninsula without meeting any resistance and captured Naples. Despite the 1495 alliance, the 'Holy League' between all of the Italian states, Germany and Spain for mutual help against France, Charles VIII's successor, Louis XII, again marched into northern Italy and claimed Milan. Here he touched on the interests of still-powerful Venice, whose exceedingly artful and commercially-minded diplomatic subterfuges had, moreover, also annoyed the other powers, the Pope and the Emperor. In 1508 an alliance therefore came into being between the Papal states, the French King Louis XII, Emperor Maximilian I, Aragon (i.e. Naples) and the Italian principalities of Urbino, Mantua and Ferrara. It was called the 'League of Cambrai'. The aggressive Pope Julius II excommunicated not only the Doge and the Government of Venice (in 1509) but also placed an interdict on the entire city. It was only before the gates of Padua, which had to be held at all costs as Venice's bridgehead into the *terra firma,* that the Venetians beat back the union troops in a final desperate effort. Only the fact that the League was suffering from internal dissensions had saved the Republic, at the last moment, from certain destruction. For almost 200 years Venice, in attack and defence, and usually against her own wishes, had been obliged to pledge mercenaries, money, and its best *condottieri* Carmagnola and Colleoni for wars and disputes on the mainland. Little wonder then that the Turks found it comparatively easy to take over Venice's last possessions and settlements in the Eastern Mediterranean, particularly since from 1520 onwards, in the person of Sultan

103

Suleiman II, the Magnificent, they were led by a shrewd Regent and an outstanding general, possessed of the fanatical religious ambition to bring Europe under the Crescent. By 1529 the Turkish land-forces stood at the gates of Vienna. The Sultan had just taken from the Order of St. John the island of Rhodes, on which Venice too had had settlements. Charles V assigned Malta to the Knights of St. John as a place of refuge. Venice now possessed only one, though the most important, outpost off the Near Eastern coast, Cyprus. Caterina Cornaro, the early-widowed wife of King James II of Lusignan, had ceded the island to Venice in 1489 in return for a small residence in Asolo, which now developed into one of the most famous artistic

104 Tintoretto: 'Mercury and the Three Graces', 1578. Venice. The Doge's Palace: Anticollegio. A painting whose composition, in three diagonally arranged figures, giving rear, frontal and profile views, appears at first sight extremely Mannerist, yet the effect of the proportioning of the bodies and their balanced relationship to one another is completely harmonious.

courts of the Renaissance. In 1566 Suleiman began the encirclement and siege of Cyprus. Nicosia fell in 1570 and Famagusta was forced to surrender in 1571. The Osmanlis had guaranteed the few surviving Venetians safe passage, but they were nevertheless slaughtered and their Commandant, Marcantonio Bragadin, flayed alive.

Only now was a cry of indignation raised throughout the Christian West. Spain, the Papacy, and Genoa, which had been watching Venice's desperate battle on Cyprus not without satisfaction, concluded a treaty with Venice on 20th May, 1571 against the Turks, who were already cruising in the Adriatic. Don John of Austria, a natural son of Charles V, was in command of the fleet which in autumn 1571 met the Turkish warships before Lepanto in the Gulf of Corinth. The Christian West, but especially Venice, whose vessels attacked first, was victorious over the Crescent. Lepanto is regarded as the greatest sea-battle ever fought in the Mediterranean and has become a legend. The Allies mourned 8,000 dead, 5,000 of them Venetians, but 25,000 Turks had lost their lives out of a total of 28,000. 'Lepanto, the last and finest victory and yet a complete defeat. Everyone of note in Venice had fought and fallen there. For nothing.' (M. Langewiesche, 1940).

Nevertheless the naval victory of Lepanto delayed the Turkish advance. Not until seventy-four years had elapsed, and while Europe was bleeding to death in the Thirty Years' War, did the Turkish fleet again put to sea, to capture Venice's last bastion, Crete (1645). For three years the Turks laid siege to Candia, the capital, which had been built up by the Veronese architect Sanmicheli, a pupil of Palladio, into one of the most formidable of fortresses. The battle became one of 'attrition', almost in the twentieth-century sense, with endless bombardments and the mining of encampments and forts. The Turks lost 120,000 men. Venice, supported by Papal troops, a handful of French nobles who had once more inscribed the ideals of the crusaders on their banner, lost 30,000 dead.

At the end of August 1669 the Commandant, Francesco Morosini, surrendered and was allowed free passage with military honours. Fourteen years later he again embarked on a final expedition against Turkey, took back the Peloponnese and founded the kingdom of the 'Morea'. The banner of St. Mark even waved for a time over Athens. Only a few years later, however, the Sublime Porte had won the territory back. After nearly three hundred years of bitter struggle Venice made peace with the Turks in Passarowitz, in 1718.

The Serenissima rewarded the last of its great commanders and admirals in 1688 with the office of Doge. As a world power, 'mistress of the seas', *a bilancia* between the great powers, Venice had no further role to play in the concert of the nations. Yet its political constitution remained, and free of political responsibility, people were still full of life and wealthy enough to dance, laugh and play throughout the century of Rococo. Goldoni and Gozzi wrote hundreds of comedies which were performed in dozens of Guardi theatres. Casanova wrote his memoirs; and Guardi and Canaletto painted the city in its prime, while Giambattista Tiepolo and his sons completed in brush and palette the last precious flowering of Venetian painting.

In 1797 Venice surrendered to the troops of Napoleon without a fight. At the Peace of Campoformio he handed the city over to Austria in exchange for Flanders and Lombardy. When the revolution opened up the notorious prisons and leaden chambers, only four common criminals were discovered. On May 12, 1797 Lodovico Manin, the 120th Doge, resigned, and placed the *cornu ducale* back in the wardrobe.

The Fine Arts

"People living in a lagoon will lack any primary relationship to architecture in stone. Even when that has been mastered, feeling for the basic tectonic relations and for balance between weight and support will not be as strong as on the mainland. The real artistic strength of lagoon inhabitants will manifest itself neither in architecture nor in sculpture but above all in painting.

Wherever light can be seen changing on the water from morning till night and soft tones link up every shape and form, painting, and especially the art of *sfumato,* is bound to feel at home.' (H. Keller, 1960).

Continuity, calm, perseverance and balanced extension, all constituent parts of Venetian state policy and the basis of its government, characterize Venice's art too, which is as closely bound up with the history of the 'Serenissima' as its geographical location. In no other Italian city were the artistic traditions and movements deriving from Eastern Rome, Byzantium, so purely preserved until the High Middle Ages. San Marco (Plates 93 and 94) is a rough copy of the Justinian Church of the Apostles in Constantinople. The system of mutually supporting cupolas, surmounted by the central cupola, is the architecturally determining factor. Not only did all Venetian churches follow this system of domed churches well into the sixteenth century, if on a smaller scale—the sole exception being the city's large Mendicant churches—but the mainland churches too were based on their great model.

Mosaic and glass-blowing probably came to Venice with the extinction of the Ravenna Exarchate. Thereafter Venice was the Italian centre for mosaic art. Artists in mosaic were dispatched from here wherever mosaics had to be laid down or renewed, to old St. Peter's in Rome for instance, in the thirteenth century. The figure hovering, incorporeal and spaceless, in front of a gold mosaic backdrop remained a feature of Venetian art for the time being, whereas in the rest of Italy the first generation of great fresco painters, Cavallini and Torre in Rome, Duccio in Siena, Giotto in Florence, Assisi and Padua, Venice's neighbour, was leaving behind the mosaic work adopted from Roman or early Christian art.

Not until 11 March 1424 did the Senate officially announce the abandonment of mosaic work. Leading Florentine painters were called to Venice: Paolo Uccello, Filipino Lippi and Andrea Castagno. They painted, *inter alia,* using the *buon fresco* technique, the rooms in the Doge's Palace and a chapel in San Zaccaria. It was thus that Venice 'came to terms' with Italian painting over a century late, caught up with it in fifty years, and by the end of the fifteenth century had not only matched Florence, Siena and even Rome, but definitely surpassed them.

Byzantine painting tradition did of course die hard. In the seventeenth century the *madonneri* still survived, who painted icons in twelfth and thirteenth century Byzantine style. Domenikos Theotocopoulos, called El Greco (1541–1614), belonged to this guild during the years of his Venetian apprenticeship.

Venice's stature in the world and her commerce, spanning continents, finally revived the sense of beauty. The material and spiritual substance available was rich enough to create a brilliant centre for all the arts, and one that would last for over three hundred years.

Painting certainly does rank first among the fine arts in Venice. The workshops and studios of Venice's painting families were based just as consciously on tradition as were the business houses and banks. For generations they were definitely family professions. *Bozzetti* (drafts), workshop instructions, pattern books, sheets of sketches and preparatory drawings for the most part remained family property. With the single exception of Giorgione, no individual name appeared in the artistic workshops in Venice. The most famous families were the Vivarini, the Bellini, with their son-in-law or brother-in-law Mantegna, the Carpaccio, Palma, Robusti (Tintoretto), Caliari (Veronese), Ricci, Longhi, Tiepolo, Guardi, Canaletto and Veccelli families (Titian was a member of the latter). After Veronese's death his brothers and sons signed the pictures 'Haeredis Paolo', 'Paolo's heirs'.

When you visit the collection of paintings in the Accademia, which were collected in a fairly random fashion, you are immediately struck by an astonishing phenomenon. The gallery is on the whole chronologically arranged and the first two rooms contain large polyptychs (altarpieces

105 Paolo Veronese: 'The Triumph of Venice', 1584. Venice. The Doge's Palace: Sala del Collegio. This oval ceiling painting is located in what is possibly the most expensively furnished room in the Doge's Palace, following the 1577 fire. It portrays 'The Triumph of Venice', 'Rei Publicae Fundamentum'. Venice Triumphant is honoured by the heavenly and earthly powers, the Virtues, Divinities of the Sea, and Patrons of the Arts. The 'Master of Perspective' has here succeeded, despite the many figures, in creating overall order by a triple-zoned architectonic arrangement.

Following pages:
106 Venice: The Rialto Bridge (Ponte di Rialto). Until the first Academy Bridge was built in 1854, this was the only bridge over the Canal Grande. It was erected from 1588 to 1591, under the direction of Antonio da Ponte, following prolonged disagreement over the designs submitted by various artists, including Palladio. A single, wide-spanned arch of Istrian marble links both banks. The passageway is traditionally lined on both sides with shops (c.f. the Ponte Vecchio in Florence), leaving only a glimpse into the central arcade. The basic form is that of all Venetian bridges: a gentle ascent, with a level area in the centre supported by the level section of the bridge's semicircular arch.

105

consisting of several panels with separate frames). They were painted by Veneziano, Jacobello del Fiore, Vivarini and Crivelli, all of them working in the Gothic manner. They all paint extremely elegant figures on a gold background which, for all their exquisite old-fashioned refinement, are often somewhat boring. You suddenly realize with amazement that most of these painters lived and died in periods when such important High Renaissance artists as Leonardo da Vinci had long since scaled their solitary peaks of artistic greatness.

Then you go into the next room, to be confronted with what is virtually mature High Renaissance art in altarpieces by Bellini, Cima da Conegliano and Montegna, and Carapaccio's richly narrative cycles from the Scuole. The use of very rich colours, blended in the most subtle way, provides a link between the two rooms, with the *sfumato* of the tonal values, even in the series of large altarpieces by various painters, thus creating a unity which seems hard to explain. It also creates a lyrical mood, with the iconographic content coming very much in second place, since the subject-matter is unique to Venetian painting.

Of the various religious innovations we will mention first the *Sacra Conversazione,* the 'Holy Conversation' between the Madonna and some of the saints. It is in fact a silent encounter, since no one speaks or even gestures. The Madonna is generally seated on a raised throne with several saints standing beside it. One of the earliest examples of this type of altar was created by a stranger, Antonio da Messina, who during his stay in Venice from 1475 to 1476 painted the Pala di San Cassiano, fragments of which are to be found to-day in the Kunsthistorisches Museum in Vienna. The real master of this genre, however, was to be Giovanni Bellini (1430–1516), younger son of Jacopo Bellini. The magic of his great altar paintings (Plate 115) lies particularly in the uncompromising stillness that seems to rule in them: a silent, solemn communing of those who understand one another without words in their 'free' and no longer earthbound sanctity. Often angels holding musical instruments are seated on the lower steps of the throne but do not play. The room in which the saints have assembled round the Madonna is sealed off to the outside world and often an aspidal flattened dome, like a protective baldaquin, full of gold mosaic work, rises above the Blessed Virgin. Only prolonged observation reveals the perfect compositional balance of these paintings.

Stillness, inaction and the absence of any relation to one another on the part of the figures represented distinguish also the paintings of Giorgione del Castelfranco, who died young, of the plague, in 1511. In barely ten years of work he so stimulated and quickened Venetian painting that even Titian found it difficult to avoid his influence. Art historical research has already ascribed nearly a hundred pictures to him, but at present his recognized and certified *oeuvre* amounts to no more than some dozen items. Giorgione introduced into the art of the lagoon city all the themes since regarded as typically Venetian. He frequented humanist circles and may have been a member of the esoteric secret societies of young Venetian nobles, probably one reason why it is difficult to interpret the content of his pictures even to-day. His mythological paintings, 'poetry', idylls, landscapes and reclining nude female figures, as well as his mysterious portraits, which say so little about the sitter, brought a new impulse to Venetian painting and one that fitted its temperament. Nearly all of his paintings were certainly commissioned by private buyers and in nearly all cases, except for the 'Castelfranco Madonna', they are small in format. His 'Tempestà' in the Accademia somehow manages to convey to us, in the smallest possible space, the manifold presence of nature.

A thunderstorm rages in the background, and flashes of lightning illuminate, in dazzling brightness, the towers and houses of a city. In the foreground, however, a woman—Madonna or gipsy?—calms her child and a youth in rather soldierly garments supports himself on a staff (or spear?). They are relaxing by a glittering stream in the midst of the reassurance of

106

P.S.I.U.P.
SI VOTA SOCIALISTA
1 RADUNO NAZIONALE
CACCIATORI ITALIANI
150

107 *Venice: View from the Campanile of the monastic island of San Giorgio Maggiore, giving a good impression of the lagoon-city's peculiar location. Only a narrow neck of land dominated by the dome of Santa Maria della Salute separates the waters of the Grand Canal from the broad Bacino and the large island, the Giudecca, behind which the wide lagoon opens.*

nature, but have no relation to each other. Everything parts them: water, meadows, a wall and the broken-off stump of a column. Atmosphere and mood, expressed chiefly in the sublime colouring, are what give the painting unity. Something similar happens with the 'Fête champêtre' (Country picnic) in the Paris Louvre. Four people, two of them men, one of whom is holding a lute, and two of them women, both nude, and all sociably disposed, are yet each isolated in a community of feeling whose absolute harmony allows of solitariness, but not loneliness.

Giorgione's 'Reclining Venus', in Dresden, is a nude but chaste feminine figure lying in an open landscape, with eyes closed, in an almost classically painted vision. This reclining nude recurs in numerous Venetian paintings, especially in Titian, and becomes a prototype which Velazquez, Goya and Manet would also feel the urge to use.

Giorgione's portraits are also veiled, to conceal their secret. 'He understands his subject as a vegetative creature and any attempt to discover character is not consistent with Giorgione's outlook. Those portrayed are not shown in action. For us they have no destiny, and no history. They manifest themselves to us only as phenomena. With such an attitude to painting it is scarcely surprising that Giorgione should have painted young people almost exclusively.' (H. Keller, 1960).

Titian, who with the portraits of Charles V, Philip II, Pope Paul III Farnese was later to become one of the most outstanding portrayers of individuals, was for a long time in his early work unable to free himself from Giorgione. 'The Knight of Malta' (Florence, Pitti Palace), the 'Young Englishman' (Munich, Ale Pinakothek) and even the 'Man with the Glove' (Paris, Louvre) remain silent and turned in upon themselves. Although Titian, 'the Prince of Painters', outshone all the other 'greats', even Leonardo and Raphael, in the eyes of his contemporaries, and was perhaps comparable to Michelangelo, who was called *il divino,* 'the divine', in his own lifetime, he remained a true son of Venice. The subdued, resonant element in his later years, visible only in the fiery glow of the gold and red in his palette; his flaky *impasto*; the deep introspection and insistent questions underlying his subject-matter, which is religious as well as mythological; the apparent stillness and quiet emanating from his most active compositions and dramatic subjects; the sudden pauses—all these features link him with Venice. Even though he was a

highly respected artist and much in demand—emperors and kings and princes were eager to own his work—he kept faith with his native city. Commissions from the Serene Republic, even from a tiny Venetian parish, were always just as important to him as those offered by world celebrities.

At a comparatively early age he was able to develop and benefit from the new self-awareness that emerged with the coming of the Renaissance. For instance on 20 March 1518, St. Bernard's Day, all the shops were closed because Titian's *Assunta,* 'The Assumption of the Virgin Mary' (plate 117), was due to be unveiled in one of the two great churches of the mendicant orders in Venice, Santa Maria Gloriosa dei Frari. Ridolfi, the painter's biographer, reports that the *curatore dell' opera* (the monk responsible for having the church built and furnished) objected to what he saw as the excessive number of saints present, saying that there was not enough room for them. And so it went on. In short, all sorts of criticisms were levelled at the painting. The emperor promptly offered to purchase it, whereupon the monks realized that 'art was not their métier and that reading their breviary did not impart any knowledge of art'. In 1548 Count Girolamo della Torre wrote to the Cardinal of Trent, who was staying in Augsburg during the Imperial Diet (to which Titian had also been invited to paint the portraits of Emperor Charles V and the Crown Prince (later King Philip II) as well as their defeated enemies), to the effect that 'the first man in Christendom [Charles V] wishes to communicate that everything possible should be done for Titian when he arrives in Augsburg in the way of comfort and convenience, and all avenues opened to him, so that he may pursue his work unhindered.'

Titian's working habits are also typical of Venetian painting, which was always concerned more with colour than with *disegno,* or drawing. We possess few, perhaps a dozen, reliably authenticated drawings by his hand. He laid his pictures directly on to the primed canvas and then—after the first few fleeting sketches, we are told—turned them to the wall, and did not turn them back again for weeks or even months, to gaze on them then like 'deadly enemies' and go on painting.

Tintoretto (1518–1594), Titian's great opposite, or counterpart, lived and worked at his side for a long time but never left Venice. He devoted himself solely to the ever greater embellishment of the palaces, churches and *Scuole* of the lagoon-city (Plates 104 and 123). If there ever was in Venice a stylistic trend

108

109

110

111

that could be called 'Mannerism', then Tintoretto was its representative. His diagonals, powerful foreshortening (either into the painting or thrusting out of it, and his unnaturally tall figures are devoid of Florentine Mannerism but inconceivable apart from the example of Michelangelo, who impressed him deeply. Above his door stood his motto: *il colorito di Tiziano, il disegno di Michelangelo*: in other words 'the colour of Titian, and Michelangelo's draughtsmanship'.

Veronese's intoxication with colour, the overwhelming development of splendour in his painting, the silken glitter and velvet glow of the garments signify the culmination of the magnificence which the state patrons wanted to see depicted. Veronese and his pupils and successors then painted the Venetian patriarchal villas on the mainland, with all the virtuosity of the *trompe l'oeil* painting whose effects still charm the beholder. Musicians sit on galleries; elegant ladies bend over balustrades; gallant gentlemen, emerging from mock doorways, greet them; while a lapdog sits on the floor in front of the framework of railings. Veronese accomplished his greatest task, however, along with Tintoretto, in painting the Doge's Palace. The residence of the Doge, the state Palace, burned down in 1577. The paintings of the Florentines who had been called to Venice at the beginning of the fifteenth century were destroyed, together with those of Pisanello from northern Italy and Titian's early work. Veronese painted one subject only, recurring in countless variations: the fame and greatness of Venice (Plate 105).

112

108 Venice: Palazzo Contarini del Bovolo: Scala del Bovolo, circa *1499. The Venetian palace 'open' system has been adopted here even for the round tower, with its spiral staircase,* Bovolo *is a Venetian dialect word for* chiociola, *'snail'.*

109, 110 and 111 Venice: Sixteenth-century palaces. This series of three palaces, erected at less than fifty-year intervals, clearly demonstrates the development of Venetian architecture. Palazzo Vendramin-Calergi (Plate 109), in which Richard Wagner died on 13.2.1883, was completed in 1509. It has a completely balanced order in which each architectural element retains its own weight. In the case of the Palazzo Corner Ca' Grande (Plate 110), erected in 1537, the heightened rusticated ground-floor assumes the function of a plinth, above which rise the two upper floors. Finally, in the Palazzo Grimani (Plate 111), built around 1550, the façade is no longer divided up symmetrically by windows and columns but is broken up into rhythmically alternating broad and narrow areas, to which the alternating arched windows correspond.

Like Tiepolo, Venice's greatest eighteenth-century master, Veronese, never painted *al fresco* in the city. Frescoes did not last in the damp air of the lagoon. Veronese's ceiling frescoes in the Doge's Palace, like those of Tintoretto in the Scuola di San Rocco, are painted on canvas. Even Tiepolo's giant painting of the 'Feast of the Rosary' in the Gesuati Church, which covers the whole of the central nave, is painted on canvas. In 1508 Titian and Giorgione were commissioned to do murals for the Fondaco dei Tedeschi on the Rialto. Just one hundred years later hardly anything could be found of this single work, which was clearly executed jointly by the two painters. The damp salt air had done its work. After that Venice was careful about frescoes, however attractively its painters worked in this form on the mainland, like Veronese at the Villa Barbaro in Maser near Treviso, or Tiepolo on the stairway of the Würzburg Court Residence.

The element of continuity in Venetian culture and the natural observance of traditions handed down, to be carried on in politics as in art, can be best understood from the matchless unity of the Piazza San Marco and the Piazzetta, that open area framed by all the important state buildings, which Napoleon rightly called 'the loveliest ballroom in Europe'. The broad S-sweep of the Canal Grande, widest and most splendid of Venetian canals, here flows into the Bacino, the city's inner harbour-basin. The earliest architectonic evidence on this square—worthy of the gem which was to be mounted there—was, and how could it be otherwise, the church of St. Mark.

114

Page 179
112 Venice: Ca' d'Oro. The palace was built between 1421 and 1440 under the direction of Bartolomeo Bon. Its beauty lies not only in the extremely rich, graceful and partly-gilded decoration of column and tracery but also in the typically Venetian manner of carrying fine filigree work over a background which is indistinguishable to the eye.

113 Andrea Mantegna: 'The Martyrdom of St. Sebastian', circa *1506. Venice: Ca' d'Oro. Mantegna, son-in-law of Jacopo and brother-in-law of Giovanni Bellini, had worked mainly in Mantua, Verona and Padua before coming to Venice. Although he was a fanatical admirer of Graeco-Roman art he nevertheless paid his own tribute to Venice in the warm tones of his later manner. The saint's body is built up in a classic* contrapposto, *like a Graeco-Roman statue, only the open mouth and eyes raised to heaven giving any indication of suffering.*

114 Venice: San Zaccaria: Façade. Like several other churches in Venice this too has a figure from the Old Testament as its patron saint, Zachariah, who is specially venerated in the Eastern Church. The façade of the well-known nunnery, which rich daughters of the Venetian Patriarchate taking the veil preferred (and purchased their way into), belongs to the second half of the fifteenth century. Both lower floors are still devoted to the Gothicizing incrustation style, but in the upper storeys and rounded gable Mauro Coducci finds his way to the great, pure, clear forms of the Renaissance.

Immediately the saint's remains had been received, a church was built for him. In the year 1073 it was decided to construct a new building worthy of him, the present domed church. It was consecrated in 1094 in the presence of Emperor Henry IV, but building continued over a period of centuries without, however, altering the basic concept (Plates 93 and 94). The church was given its richest enhancement at the beginning of the thirteenth century, when the mosaics in the vestibule (or narthex) were completed, and the building decorated with items of booty from Constantinople—hundreds of columns, capitals, reliefs and mural facings of the finest marble, the most valuable pieces being brought to the south side of the church, which faces the Piazzetta and the sea. Even to-day this is the side that appears like a collection of trophies to the greater glory of the saint and the Serene Republic. No feeling

115 Giovanni Bellini: 'Sacra Conversazione'. ('Madonna and Child with Saints'), 1505. Venice: San Zaccaria. This is perhaps the richest of Bellini's portrayals of the Sacra Conversazione. *The Madonna, enthroned, is holding the upright Christ-child on her left knee. An angel at her feet on the steps of the throne is playing a musical instrument. On her right are St. Peter and St. Catherine; on her left, St. Jerome and St. Lucy. There is no communication between the personages, not so much as a glance. Each is quite self-contained. And yet in a higher sense they are bound together by their inner peace, the harmony of the composition and the protective mosaic baldaquin, whose painted architectonic perspective exactly corresponds to the 'built-in' altar-frame.*

116 Venice: Santa Maria dei Miracoli: Detail of Ceiling Decoration. This little church was built between 1481 and 1489 by Pietro Lombardo and his school from the finest, delicately-coloured and shaded marble. The panelled ceiling, consisting of curves and straight lines, is a lovely example of early Venetian ceiling decoration.

116

for symmetry determines the order in which they are arranged, as in the Classical Period or the Renaissance. They are distributed over the façade in a trophies, the two 'Tetrarchs', a porphyry group of two Regents embracing, seemingly arbitrary manner, their importance being indicated by the position they occupy in reference to the church interior. The most precious which dates from the fourth century A.D.—porphyry was considered a royal stone, so that only Emperors had statues made of it—is situated at the corner of the south side, at the exact spot where the Treasury is located on the inside.

S. GREGORIO
BARBARIGO
S. GERARDO
SAGREDO

118

117 Titian: 'Assumption of the Blessed Virgin' ('Assunta'), 1518. Venice: Santa Maria Gloriosa dei Frari: High Altar. With this gigantic altar-painting (6.90 metres × 3.60 metres) (22' 6" × 11' 7") Titian created the prototype of the high altar-painting that remained the rule up into the High Baroque period and perhaps even for Rubens. However solidly arranged the separate groupings—the astonished and terrified Apostles around the grave, the Blessed Virgin surrounded by an angelic halo, and God the Father receiving her—the factor determining the pictorial structure is its colour composition, the guiding lines of the red tones, in their gradations.

118 and 119 Venice: Scuola Grande di San Marco. The façade of this scuola*, which is now the Venice municipal hospital, was erected between 1485 and 1495. It is a masterpiece of Venetian Early Renaissance architecture, for the wealth of its coloured marble incrustation, and particularly its subtly illusionary effects in the matter of perspective. Two lions, a reference to the name of the school, seem to emerge right and left of the main portal (Plate 119). At the side, the façade joins up with the second large church of the Mendicant Orders after the Frari, Santi Giovanni e Paolo.*

119

This corner also forms the main entrance to the Doge's Palace, the Porta della Carta, so the 'Tetrarchs' clearly represent the interlocking nature of Venice's secular and spiritual power.

The main façade on the Piazza is one of the later sections, with its five round portals leading into the narthex—the central one being higher than the others. Over them is the surrounding gallery, and above that the high, wide and rounded arches bear mosaics which are framed by white marble canopies, small spires and crockets in the Late Gothic flamboyant style. Their flowery tendrils, like petrified Burano lace, creep round the gold mosaic work. The broad West Window in the central area is almost hidden by the powerful four-in-hand bronze horses, the most precious part of the Byzantine booty, fourth or third century B.C. Greek work and the only bronze *Quadriga* to survive from the ancient world.

The next structure to be built in the Piazza and Piazzetta ensemble was what the Venetians affectionately call the *paron de casa* (the Head of the House), the Campanile (Plate 107), linking the two squares like a hinge. It rises to a height of 95 metres (313′ 6″) on a square that is 12 metres × 12 metres (39′ × 39′). Construction was begun in the ninth century and concluded in 1517, when it was crowned by a three metre (9′ 9″) high gilded statue of the Archangel Gabriel. This figure, visible for miles, guided ships by day into the Bacino. On stormy nights a beacon-fire was lit in the bell-loft. The Campanile's particular attractiveness rests finally on two factors, apart from its extremely simple but splendidly-conceived articulation. These factors are, firstly, the colour alternations between the dull dark red brick and the crystalline, light-catching transparency of the white marble; and secondly, the harmonious balance between the horizontal and vertical elements. The soaring upwards surge of the proud, steep pilaster strips is held in check throughout by the weight of the heavy marble cornices. With a subtle feeling for the pressure of tracery the cube is gradually eased and reduced. More decorative forms, small columns in the round arched arcade of bell-storey and the balustrade arrangement, then subsume the vertical movement, which finally seems to flow with the steep pyramid roof and crowning statue of the angel into the lagoon itself. In the early hours of 14 July 1902 the Campanile collapsed. Miraculously no one was injured and the neighbouring structures suffered little or no damage. Nine months later, in April 1903, reconstruction was begun, and lasted nine years.

The Doge's Palace (Plates 93, 98,100–103), the seat of government, was given its present form in the fourteenth and fifteenth centuries; the south side, on the Mole and sea, in the fourteenth; and the section adjoining the Piazzetta in the late fifteenth century Gothic period. The façades of the Palace even today reveal in the purest form Venice's peculiar attitude to architecture, which never favours what is static. To some extent the closed wall of the upper storey rests on the elegant column of the lower arcaded floor and the first floor above it, which is concealed behind a delicate curtain of colonnades, with Gothic tracery in the spandrels. Yet this high, wide area is again so gently articulated, merely by the change from the bright red and white of the stone cover, that the resulting textile-like ornamentation resembles patterned material rather than a solid wall.

Numerous fires kept plaguing the Palace, one of the severest (1483) destroying, *inter alia,* the first great painting cycles, in the interior, by the Florentine painter Pisanello. In 1577 the exterior was badly damaged and the entire treasury of paintings carried out during the High Renaissance, on commission from the state, fell victim to the flames. Tintoretto and Veronese, with their pupils, repainted the rooms (Plates 102–105) in the shortest possible time. The exterior—although Palladio hastened to put forward new plans for modernization, which were in accordance with his classical taste—was restored in its old form. On the Piazza north of San Marco rises the 'Torre del Orologio', the Clock Tower, built by Mauro Coducci and decorated with richly coloured marble incrustations (Plates 96 and 97). Today the two *mori,* bronze human figures, still strike the hours with their hammers on the big bell.

120

120 Venice: San Michele in Isola: Façade. The church of Venice's island cemetery—lying in the lagoon some 800 metres (870 yards) from the mainland—was constructed by Mauro Coducci from 1469 onwards. In structure it is distinctly reminiscent of the façade of San Zaccaria, which is also by Coducci (c.f. Plate 114).

121

121 Andrea Verrocchio: Equestrian Monument of Condottiere Bartolomeo Colleoni, 1481–1488. Venice. Campo San Giovanni e Paolo. This most famous of Italian Renaissance equestrian statues, along with Donatello's 'Gattamelata' in Padua, was created between 1481 and 1488 by the Florentine sculptor and painter Andrea Verrocchio. A high plinth raises the bronze figure—which is executed in the most naturalistic manner, as is evident from the Condottiere's face or the decoration on the reins—away from the yellow-brown of the church walls and to some extent higher than normal, thus elevating the field-commander to 'a gladiatorial dominance'. (E. Hubala).

The entire north side of the Piazza, up to a length of 152 metres (501′ 7″), was soon afterwards taken up by the Procuratie Vecchie, the Residence of the Procurators of San Marco (Plate 95). Though on the threshold of the Renaissance, this structure still retains the Byzantine-Gothicizing style of the Doge's Palace, with its graduated series of three arcades and arched windows.

Not until the Libreria Marciana, the Library, was built on the Western side of the Piazzetta, opposite the Doge's Palace, by Jacopo Sansovino (1488–1570) did the High Renaissance make its brilliant debut in these squares (Plate 93). 'Both storeys of the Library, built from 1537 from his [Sansovino's] design, are constructed on the illustrationary type of Tabularium motif, the lower floor follows the Doric, and the upper the Ionic order. The concluding . . . frieze with the putti bearing garlands, in imitation of classical fragments of reliefs, parades its Roman origin.' (J. Burckhardt, 1855).

The Library is still a piece of Venetian architecture, however, and not merely because of its rich decoration. The articulation of the second floor is un-Roman, in that the round arched opening has not been shaped and proportioned as a pillared arcade after the solid building style, but as an open colonnade, and is therefore in the Venetian tradition. And since these arches supported by paired columns are linked by short straight architrave sections to pillars behind the great columns, we arrive at the richest articulation motif in Italian art, the 'Serlio' or Palladio motif: 'The columned arcade in the centre is flanked by two colonnaded sections . . . Wherever a living reflection of plastic values was striven after, resource was had to this type of composition.' (E. Habala, 1968). Sansovino's architectural system was essentially retained in the *Procuratie Nuove,* erected from 1584 under the direction of Palladio's pupil, Vincenzo Scamozzi, on the south side of Piazza San Marco.

It was left to Napoleon to close the square by building up the west side. In 1807 a church was torn down on his orders, and the classical 'Ala Napoleonica', the Napoleon wing, was erected, based on the form of the two Procuratorates. The city's noblest work of art was thus completed simultaneously with Venice's demise as a political power.

122 Venice: Isola di San Giorgio Maggiore. The monastic island of the Benedictines owes its architectural appearance to-day largely to sixteenth century extensions and conversions, especially the reconstruction of the church, begun in 1566 by Andrea Palladio. The interior and façade of San Giorgio Maggiore became models not only in Upper Italy for many seventeenth and eighteenth century religious buildings. Though a first glance reveals the overall classical structure of the façade, yet the multistoreyed orders are highly artistically combined in mutual dependence.

122

It is not only in the area of St. Mark's Square that Venice's image has been left untouched, a rare stroke of fortune in today's world. The great churches of the Mendicant Orders too, such as Santa Maria dei Frari and Santi Giovanni e Paolo ('San Zanipolo'), with Palladio's religious buildings (Frontispiece, Plate 122), and above all the palaces along the Canal Grande, have come down to us as intact groupings. A detailed examination of the art of Venetian palace architecture from the thirteenth to the eighteenth century would exceed the limits of our survey, so rich are their forms of decoration, despite the fact that they are all based on the same morphological principles. A charming way of spending the time is to drift along the Grand Canal in a boat, seeing how the very different palace façades are in fact variations on a single theme and thus receiving a lesson in architectural style—from the Ca'd'Oro (1421–1440) past the Palazzo Contarini del Bovolo (circa 1500) to the Palazzo Vendramin-Calergi (1509) and the Palazzo Corner Ca' Grande (1537) or the Palazzo Grimani (1550) (Plates 108–112). These all have one thing in common, even as early as the thirteenth century, the wide, hospitable, inviting façade opening outward on to the Canal, a unique feature in medieval secular architecture. The central opening was often at water-level, permitting

123 Tintoretto: 'The Last Supper', 1594. Venice. San Giorgio Maggiore. Presbytery. This 'Last Supper' is the final version of a theme which Tintoretto often treated in Venetian churches. When Christ pronounced the words: 'One of you will betray me', the disciples leapt to their feet in great excitement. The deep diagonal line of the table underlines the drama of the event. The pictorial effect depends however on the flickering gleams of luminosity in which the figures of angels flash forth.

124 Venice: Canal Grande, evening. Timbered jetties thrusting their way out of the water and the gaily-painted poles for tying up the gondolas belong, like the gondolas themselves, to the unmistakeable image of Venice.

the gondola to enter the interior of the house. *Piazza*, canal and street work their way in the freest and most open manner into the concealing four walls, providing an insight into the essence of the medieval city.

Companionship was a feature of Italian towns, an untiring need to communicate and to exchange information and opinions in a free and easy manner, in the *piazza,* across the yard, or from window to window. In their open structures, the 'familiar' order of church, palace and town-hall, or of loggia, market and monastery, around the square or ordered in a roadway, they embody the free and inquiring spirit that has been a governing factor since the late Middle Ages, a spirit which the modern visitor feels here, and the Italian traveller of the Middle Ages looked to as an alternative to the walled-in confines and political repression of the medieval world, an ideal image of free human intercourse beneath a bright serene sky, whose indulgent climate made it possible to go out or in, from *piazza* to salon, or street to corridor. It is no coincidence that the architectural theory of the Italian Renaissance defined the house as a town in miniature, and the town as a 'house' writ large, and equated *sala* and *piazza.*

Bewitched by the perfection of organically evolved structures, the open-minded traveller in Rome, Florence or Venice finds the basic human needs of unrestricted communication and free social intercourse reflected in architectural creations which even in their most monumental form do not turn away from but towards each other, and relate not to themselves but to something outside. The public buildings, like the private buildings of the ruling class, express power, but seldom excessive power; self-awareness but seldom self-aggrandizement. The free citizen's right to exist remained largely untouched by these architectural signs of power. Nowhere did the townsman liberate himself earlier or more consistently into a freer, self-conscious political existence than in the Italian *commune* of the fourteenth to sixteenth centuries, or find his way towards a social identity which was soon directed against the relics of medieval domination. It was logical, therefore, that at the end of the Renaissance the upper classes had to bear the brunt of city hostility. They returned to the feudal framework of the country, the castle, the manor, the villa, from which, centuries before, they had crowded into the towns. When the Italian aristocracy retired to the insularity of their *villegiature* from about 1500 to 1550, with the 'Phantom of *piazza*, *commune* and Cathedral, and the faces of lurking friends and laughing enemies before their eyes.' (R. Borchardt), they turned their back not just on the city but on a freedom which was no longer theirs alone.